OUR OWN WORST ENEMY

A True Portrait of Black America

Revised Edition

David G. Bowman

authorHOUSE®

AuthorHouse™
1663 Liberty Drive
Bloomington, IN 47403
www.authorhouse.com
Phone: 1-800-839-8640

First published by AuthorHouse 5/24/2010

ISBN: 978-1-4208-3109-2 (sc)

Library of Congress Control Number: 2010907461

Printed in the United States of America
Bloomington, Indiana

This book is printed on acid-free paper.

Cover design by: Ervin Toliver.

This book in its entirety is dedicated to the memory of my mother Beryl Jean Bowman Lanier (1929 - 1990) and my stepfather, L.J. Lanier (1930 - 2001).

I would like to thank my wife Doris Toliver Bowman for all of the support in which she has given me in the writing of this book.

A special thank you to two of my high school teachers, Mr. Percy Brown and Mrs. Betty Lou Brown (not related) for believing in me when no one else did. Also my fourth grade teacher, Mrs. Molly Buck, for giving me the lead role in our end-of-school play because she knew that I could do it.

I would also like to say thank you to my six children, Terrance, Danel, Russell, LaKeytra, Temerica, and Adrieanna.

My sincere gratitude goes out to Kevin and Karen Warner (brother & sister) for their assistance with the revision of this book.

TABLE OF CONTENTS

INTRODUCTION

The reason for my writing a book of this magnitude is to inspire black Americans to take a thorough self-assessment of themselves. This is a book that should be opened and read not only for black Americans. I invite other races to understand the history and culture of my people. I truly believe that God holds each and every one of us accountable for our deeds toward one another. Jesus said, "I am giving a new commandment to you now, love each other just as much as I love you. (John 13:34).

I have no intentions of demeaning or demoralizing my people in any shape, form, or fashion because that was already done before me and my readers were born. However, I must tell the whole truth in hopes of shedding light upon our self-applied downfalls as well as the systemic low expectations and discrimination that occur today. Regardless of what the dominant group believes and does, we must become a determined race of people. Even though racism and discrimination do exist, it is time we overcome those obstacles and take responsibility for our own destiny. This requires some creativity and hard work, but there is no other way to approach our self-inflicted or society-inflicted problems within the black race. If we always do what we've always done, we'll get what we always got almost nothing!

The biggest problem for black Americans is between their two ears: their thinking. It is imperative that we change our way of thinking lest we perish. The first way to make this change is by changing our entire approach toward racism by using that energy towards the upward mobility of our race. Doing this will impact future generations.

Another major challenge is regaining the control of our youth. We have lost at least 35 percent of the last three generations of black youth, and that's being conservative. In the words of Dr. John Henrik Clarke, black parents have adopted the sociology of the dominant race insofar as rearing children. I pray that every parent – fathers as well as mothers – stand accountable for the way they rear their children. After all, the foundation of society is the home where the parent(s) should be in total control.

The fact that black people are the only race of people that did not come to America under their own free will is quite significant. We were brought here unwillingly and in chains on the slave ship *Jesus*. Black people were brought to America so that the Europeans could become rich and live life leisure. We were put to work in fields with no wages. We were abused culturally, physically, mentally, verbally, emotionally, sexually, and economically. We were, no doubt, wronged by these abuses. Nevertheless, we can take the brutality of our past to beautify our future.

The irony of the name of the slave ship should be inspiration enough for us to set records in areas other than sports. We can work together as one people in order to regain our historical dignity and nobility.

Black history has been offered as an *elective* in public schools. Until parents realize the satanic scheme of the suppression of Negro history, black history, and African American history, they will continue to buy fireworks for the 4th of July, failing to realize that on the 4th of July, 1776 (Independence Day) blacks were in slavery. When blacks celebrate the 4th of July, they are simply perpetuating the lie-- Americans are one big equal family. We can revolutionize the world. We can shake up the world by commanding the respect of society. This can be done *in God we trust.*

CHAPTER ONE

THE WHITE MAN SYNDROME

All things are decided by fate; it was known long ago what each man would be. So there is no use arguing about your destiny. (Ecclesiastics 6:14).

The white man is only as powerful as the black man believes him to be. Some of us tend to place blame on the white man instead of being responsible for our own actions. Black America no longer has the luxury of using the white man as an excuse for their failures.

It is now time for black America to take a serious at ourselves! It is past time for us to redeem ourselves and our once prideful place in the United States of America. We must go back to who we once were. We were once a race of people who placed a tremendous value on spirituality and family above all else. In fact, we had spirituality before Christ was born. We knew that someone was in charge of things like the weather and the world around us. Black Americans have earned the right to be here. We have only to take our rightful place and become a more productive race of people in this country. It is time for some of us to stop making excuses and start making progress. Either we can become part of the solution or continue to be a vast part of the problem. Some of us have got to stop looking the other way and start accepting responsibility for our problems. Many blacks have depended too long upon the white man to solve our problems, blaming the white race for our failure to determine our own destiny. In reality it is God who decides our fate, not the white man.

If the white race is to be blamed for our failures, then in all fairness, we must give them the credit for our success. It's like some of us are giving white America control over our lives. I, too, have blamed the white race for every downfall in which I have been responsible for. I had always used my being black as an excuse for my failures in the past. It always seemed the easiest way out for me and many other black Americans, for we did not want to accept the fact that we were – and some of us still are – a self-destructing people. Until we could admit to ourselves that only we can determine the outcome of our own lives, we will remain troubled as a people.

Some blacks live in rundown ghettos simply because we choose to live there. Many of us make less money than our white counterparts simply because we settle for less. These particular black Americans are not willing to put forth any extra effort in order to achieve more for their families and themselves. The problem will not simply go away without effort, and we cannot solve them overnight.

The unsuccessful black Americans have only to seek the solution within them-selves. Only then will they find the answer and move forward as a people.

There will always be the white man, and I'm sure that there will always be prejudice and discrimination in some form. Prejudice nor discrimination will not go away anytime soon; at least not during any of our lifetimes. However, we must at least be willing to work hard at overcoming its evils in order to gain an equal share of what America has to offer us.

I am not asking my people to give up their pride, but be willing to overcome the "white man syndrome" or whatever else is holding them back. I am not trying to put down my own race, nor am I suggesting that we are inferior in any way to any race of people on this planet. I am, however, determined to overcome my "black" way of thinking. I refuse to continue to carry the white man around in my head! I realize I must place God above all else and believe that I can do all things through Him. I promise that all obstacles will be removed in due season.

The white man is not a threat to us unless we truly believe that he is! The only way anyone can stop black America is for us to stop ourselves. We can actually be anything we want to be in this great country. We have got to believe that equal rights are for all of us today. There are mandated federal laws to protect these rights. The highest court in America declared these laws constitutional. Now we must pursue true fulfillment and success in the United States of America.God created all men equal, not just according to the *Constitution*.

According to God, prejudice against people for being different existed even during the time of Jesus. In Matthew 15: 22-28, a woman from Canaan was desperate and went to Jesus for help. She knew that this Man of God would help her. Jesus did not turn her away even though the people from Canaan were accustomed to prejudice. This woman was despised and ridiculed because of prejudice, but she believed in Jesus. She accepted being treated differently because she was from Canaan. You see, Jesus died for not only our sins; he died also for the sins of the white man. Jesus died for the sins of those who enslaved my ancestors as well. Slavery is what brought us to America, and it is up to black Americans to make the best of that fact. It is not how we got here; it is what we have done after our rights were given to us and we became full citizens of America.

Black Americans must forgive those who once held us in bondage and live for the many slaves who died without ever knowing what it felt like to be free as we are today. Now is the time to let go of what others have done to our race in the past. We must know our history but hold no grudges. We must forgive but never forget all the lives that slavery has cost our people who fought for the freedom in which black Americans enjoy today. Both blacks and whites have paid a dear price for black Americans to have equal right, but many are not taking full advantage of becoming the proud race of people that we were meant to be.

It is not too late to save the dignity of our race, and it is not too late to save our race from self-destruction by any means. If some blacks continue to regress, then all of those who fought for our freedom will have died in vain. Some of us are our own worst enemy and will be until we go back to our African roots. We must again become a people who are hungry for freedom. We must dance the dance of progress to the beat of the old African drums of our forefathers. We must live up to our capabilities and strive to get the most out of ourselves. We must become a proud people once again and set out together in order to solve our own problems within our own race.

We must let go of hate and allow God to bring about prosperity among our people. Black America has only to look in the mirror in order to see who the enemy really is. Some of us are destroying ourselves, but there is still a chance to repair the damage some of us have caused with in our race.

We have begun a new millennium. We as black Americans should be very concerned about our future in this country. I know for a fact that many blacks do not believe in themselves enough to overcome poverty nor escape the life of the inner city. We are, for the most part, responsible for what the inner city has become. We are convinced that the white man puts the drugs in the hands of our children and forces them to sell and use. We have become so narrow minded until we can't see the forest for the trees.

I realize that there are many successful blacks in the world today. However, it is because of ambition and a desire to compete with the white race in the real world. Those of us who remain in the ghetto are the ones who believe in an all black society of self-regressing people who don't want anything out of life. Those are the people who are dead before they die. No one has to spend his or her entire life in the ghetto. Not all people in poor black inner city areas are deadbeats, but there are those who make their own rules outside the law in which they refer to as "the white man's law". They do not understand that the rest of the world is progressing while they are regressing.

Allow me to explain something in which God gave me to share with you. We do not have to like what was done to us in the past, and we do not have to like what is being done to us today. We do, however, have to love our oppressors just as God loves us. I am not saying you have to like what a person has done to you, but you have to love that person in order for you to be blessed by God. I have been in the hood myself, and I've lived in the world of the black man. I have sold drugs and used drugs as if it were lawful to do so.

I have become very concerned about what will become of the black race within the next one hundred years. If we continue at our present pace, our regression will also continue as well. How can we survive another one hundred years of not getting better as a race? Yes, some of us will undoubtedly continue to be successful. However, that number will be too small to make a realistic change in our regression. The few blacks who do achieve their goals because of hard work and determination will not, by any means, be able to support an entire race. There are far too many unproductive black Americans.

A change has to be made in each of us in order for a struggling race to even begin to show progress of any kind.

A famous comedian once said, "Black people will become extinct, and the only blacks you'll see will be in museums." Now that statement may be a bit farfetched, but it gives us something to think about. I don't understand why most blacks seem to be afraid of change. We have to want crime and drugs out of our neighborhoods. We do not need to be concerned about what the white man won't do to help us clean up our streets. We are beginning to weaken as a people because we seem not to care about how or where we live. Some are quick to point the finger instead of being held accountable for our own actions. May God be with the black man for the next one hundred years and beyond – if we can hold on that long!

It has become a way of life for low income blacks to fail. We have got to learn not to accept failure as a part of everyday living in the ghetto. It becomes very easy for us to give up instead of working hard, striving to achieve our goals. Some black Americans tend to lack the will to work hard to get whatever we may want or need. Some blacks have become unafraid to fail but afraid of change. We must learn to embrace change with all our might and strength so that we can do better for ourselves. We may be afraid of failure in the sense that we will be held accountable for our failures. We become failures simply by not acknowledging our setbacks.

Many blacks make excuses for not being in the mainstream of successful America. We blame others for what we won't do for ourselves and refuse to accept responsibility for failing. We have, for the most part, become an envious and self-righteous people who can't stand to see members of our race succeed. We, at times, seem to be ashamed of who we are and where we came from. Some of us have become whitenized, not worrying about the white man, but trying to emulate him. For example, our hair is naturally kinky (curled at the root). Some straighten their hair with harsh chemicals. Some lengthen their hair with glued in hair or sewn in weaves. In fact, some put weaved hair in layaway just so they can afford it.

The white race has always been known to help each other. They pass on helpful information in order to aid a family member, friend, or coworker. It is not a crime to aid a member of your race. That is the reason why white Americans are able to maintain a step ahead of black Americans. It is not that whites are better than blacks. They are just more organized. In order for us to become organized also, we must work together toward the very same goals. We must make an attempt to reclaim our heritage.

Progress will not take place for us unless we are willing to achieve it by working as one people. We cannot give up on becoming a better people. We must first set short-term goals. Then as time goes by, we will be able to accomplish long-term goals. America is the "melting pot" for all races of people, and it is solely up to black Americans to reap the riches of this nation. We must first learn to love each other. Secondly, we must learn to love outside our race, regardless of circumstances. Only then can we overcome racism.

The white man is not a problem to us unless we continue to consider him to be a problem. Racism is not our biggest problem. The real problem is drugs, crime, and irresponsibility for the actions of our black children. Now is the time for us to be freed from the white man syndrome once and for all.

CHAPTER TWO

PROGRESS THROUGH EDUCATION

Gaining wisdom is the most important goal that one can accomplish! Along with your new found wisdom comes the development of common sense and good judgment. If you exalt wisdom, she will exalt you. Hold her fast, and she will lead you to great honor; she will place a beautiful crown upon your head. My people, listen to me, and do as I say, and you will have a long, good life. (Proverbs 4: 7-10).

I truly believe that the future of black America begins with our children receiving an education in hope that they will gain wisdom. Whenever I drive by an elementary school and see little children in the schoolyard playing together, I can't help but notice how well these children get along together regardless of skin color. There is an important lesson to be learned by parents. Those very same children would grow up loving one another if only parents would not poison their innocent little minds with racism. This is not the type of education that we need for our children. Children do not see color nor know to hate someone who is different unless foolish grownups teach them. Jesus said, "Suffer little children, and forbid them not to come unto Me, for such is the kingdom of heaven" (Matthew 19:14).

The greatest gift that a parent can give a child is wisdom by way of an education. We must realize how impressionable a little child must be, and it has got to be a sin before God to teach a child to hate another child because of skin color. Integration and equal education is the best thing that has ever happened for black Americans. We have also gained the right to vote. Now our children can sit in the very same classroom as white children and receive an equal education. Equal education is very important to the progression of our race. Equal education gives black children an equal chance to compete on the same level with any race. Black and white children can now play and work together with the very same skills. So, there shouldn't be any reason why our children can't grow up together and live in this big world upon equal terms. It can only happen if parents would allow children to be children and love each other.

May God bless the children of this world to love one another for who they are and not by whatever color their skin may happen to be! The children of today will become teachers, lawyers, and presidents. They are the future of this nation and of our race. I know for a fact that educated black children can make it better for all of us. This world is a great big playground for all races of children. There is no reason why it cannot become a friendly circus when they grow up. After all, such as them is the kingdom of heaven, according to Christ Jesus.

There is not reason why black Americans cannot increase the number of educated members of our race. There isn't one single reason why blacks can't achieve as much or more than our white counterparts. There is no reason in the world why we don't own more land, have more college's degrees, and move out of slum areas. I cannot accept the reasons why we are moving backward instead of progressing forward. Some of us are being set back because we do not place value upon the importance of an equal education. We are solely responsible for our own decisions, and it's high time for us to own up to who we have become today.

Not even God will help a people – regardless of race – who don't have the desire to help themselves. We are destroying all that our ancestors have worked and died for. Our ancestors died for us to overcome the hardships in which we endure today. We were brought to this country in order to work as field hands and servants for white people. However, we cannot harbor that dark piece of history forever. We understand just what it feels like to work for unfair wages, and most of us know what it is like not to make enough money in order to adequately take care of our children. We have been, for the most part, always at the rear of the line all of our lives here in the United States; but it really doesn't have to be that way anymore. We do not have to be poor or last because we are not slaves anymore. We are free to do anything that white folks do. We must take pride in who we are, and become more educated.

More blacks must gain access to computers in their homes for their families. We must update our education into the 21st century. We must learn to deal with our problems in a civil manner. We must learn to deal with racism and not allow ignorance to set us back any further than we are now. We have a need to exercise every right in which the *Constitution* of this country allows us under the laws of this nation. We cannot continue to waste any more time crying over the spilled milk of our past. It is time to follow Dr. Martin Luther King's strategy of nonviolence and become a well-respected race of people. This endeavor will not only be won by the strongest, but the most educated. We are already equal to any race in the world. It is time to live up to that fact. In Matthew 5:9, Jesus said, "Blesses are the peace makers, for they shall be called the children of God." Black people have been called everything but the children of God. So why, all of a sudden, get in an uproar when we are called names by other races. We can either move on or remain at the end of the line of progress. Remember that it takes God, education, and wisdom in order for us to get ahead in this world. Now I ask you to maintain an open mind while reading the rest of this chapter so that you can fully understand the importance of a good education.

During slavery, black people were not allowed to learn how to read. If a slave was caught with a book of any kind in his or her possession, including the *Bible*, it may have caused that slave to lose his or her life. White slave owners knew even back then that if a slave could learn how to read, then slaves would eventually know as much as whites. Now, that is a powerful message to think about. The same applies today in the sense of educated blacks becoming a bigger part of the corporate world and gaining more political power. I want black America to feel me on what I am saying. Again I want to stress the fact that white people have known for years about the unlimited powers of an education.

There isn't anyone to stop us from learning all of the secrets of the entire universe through education but ourselves. It is our choice to receive what is long due us, and that is the chance to become productive people in any job market. As for myself, I am an honor graduate of the prestigious school of "hard knocks". I majored in making my life hard for myself. I didn't have the luxury of having a white man to aid me in almost ruining my life because I did a good job on my own defects. The white man was not with me when I sold and used drugs. The white man was nowhere

9

around when I went to jail. He was not present when I quit college. So, how can I blame anyone but myself? It was not the white society who was responsible for my bad decisions. Therefore, the white society cannot take credit for my recovery. I thank Jesus for who I have become today and for giving me the wisdom to not only help myself; but to share my wisdom with other black Americans.

You see if I had not gone through that which God has allowed me go to through – both good and bad – then there would be no way possible for me to have written this book. You may have never come to terms with the truth. God allowed me to take this path in order for me to guide my people in the direction of honor and truth toward progress. I realize that I am a long way from being perfect. However, I have grown wiser, and I thank my Lord and Savior that I am not the man I once was! I want very much to help blacks understand the importance of receiving an equal education. Once you've received an education, you must become a productive member of black America. We must understand that there is a need for a productive black America in order for us to receive any recognition or positive results from within our ranks.

We must change our aggressive behavior toward white America and change our approach to racism. Education will help change our black way of thinking. We must learn to compete with our white friends on their turf and on their terms. The only way to do this is for more blacks to become educated. We won't start progressing until we can stop regressing, and we won't stop sinking until we start thinking. Please take heed to what I am saying to you and understand that I am on your side.

I am black, and I have lived among my black peers all of my life. I have taken parts in conversations with black people all of my life as well. We are too concerned about everything except what is going on with us. Even when we go to football games, we tend to think that when the team on the field is in the huddle, they are talking about black people. (I say that for a joke because we could really use a laugh right about now). I realize that there's got to be a better way than what we believe. Many blacks are worry about the wrong things. We can't solve everyone's problems; we should focus on solving our own.

I will never forget where I came from. Neither will I forget all that my mother went through rearing 9 children. I will always remember all of the young black men I left behind in prison. My heart goes out to those who are on the street with no place to go. I think about those who I got high with who are still getting high today, and I realize that I am still no better than any of them. The only difference is that I wanted a better life for myself and my family. I stress to my children the importance of an education. I teach them that education will overcome discrimination most of the time. I now demand more from myself and from my children. Everyone is capable of rendering such sound changes, but the changes have to come because you want them, not need them. Those of us who are of sound mind must help our brothers and sisters who want to be helped and are willing to help themselves.

Black Americans have not suffered enough to realize that there is a better life awaiting those of us who desire it. Desire will soon mature into a butterfly of ambition in which will blossom one day into progress and success. Progress may start only one inch at a time, but in time it will become a mile of success for our race. It all starts with education. There a many black single mothers who are going back to school. Welfare has helped them to pay for daycare for their children. Yet, there are still some black mothers who are solely dependent upon the welfare system and are not seeking any kind of job to support their children. Welfare has become a problem oftentimes toward the progression of black America. Welfare is a roadblock to education, self-esteem, pride, and progression.

Many young black mothers have grown accustomed to sitting at home waiting for a low income, monthly welfare check, which is referred to as "Mothers Day" by drug dealers. Some mothers do need assistance in order to care for their babies, but many are seeking a handout from hardworking Americans. I promise you the whole truth, and so you shall receive that truth as promised to you. I can understand that a young lady can make a mistake and have a child out of wedlock, thus, becoming a single parent who needs welfare. However, while unmarried and on welfare, why have another child, then another, then another, then another under the very same circumstances and not seek a job for support?

Our children are learning the same easy way out from their single, jobless mothers. President Bill Clinton has made it possible for those receiving welfare to continue their education, therefore, giving single mothers a choice. Now everyone on welfare can begin to experience workfare. It is only fair to work as other Americans do. Go to school, learn a skill, or receive a degree of some kind instead of welfare. You can fare well in life.

Black women are very capable of sustaining a reasonable living for themselves without a man to help out. I am talking about the strong-willed black women who do not depend upon welfare to give them a handout. Our progress will have to depend heavily upon these women in the 21st century to raise the moral standards of our entire race. Black American women have been abused since the start of slavery and even more so today by no one other than the black man. Nevertheless, these women still depend on an inner strength that somehow keeps them going against all odds. There is no one more ambitious than an educated black woman. We must seek progress by using the black woman as our inspiration. After all, it was the black woman who gave birth to the black man in the first place. They carried us in their wombs for 9 months, and they are still carrying us today.

CHAPTER THREE

BLACK PARENTS

We as black parents must become a positive role model for our children by setting good examples in the way we live. Black parents must teach their children by showing them how to live a life that is approved by God. We do not just have a black youth problem. We have a young black parent problem as well. We have got to educate our young parents to be good parents.

"And now a word to you parents; this is the right thing to do, don't keep on scolding and nagging your children, making them angry and resentful. Rather, bring them up with the loving discipline himself approves, with suggestions and Godly advice." (Ephesians 6:4) I was 11 or 12 years of age when I was forced to help at my father's mechanic shop. I helped out every day except Sundays. My stepfather worked me so hard at times that I thought he didn't like me, but now I realize that he was only teaching me to work and to be responsible. He would always tell me not to ever sit down on the job. I have passed this same lesson on to my three boys.

Russell is the youngest of the three, and at the age of 14 he worked with a janitorial service every chance he was given the opportunity. Russell knows the importance of working for what he wants and realizes that work is a part of life. There isn't any doubt in my mind that Russell will achieve all of his goals in life. He has established himself a good foundation and is about to enter college soon.

Black parents must encourage their children and, at the same time, leave the door open in order to learn about your child's character. None of us as parents are perfect, and we sometimes learn as we rear our children. Set goals with your children because they are never too young to start thinking about who or what they will become. Children may change their minds from time to time, but at least they will be giving some thought about their future. It is always good to talk to your children about their intentions concerning their adult lives. Offer them suggestions but, most importantly, listen to what your child has to say. Even when Russell was only 14 years of age, I learned an awful lot about myself just from listening to him.

When I was 14 years of age, I would daydream of Tom Sawyer and Huckleberry Finn sailing down the mighty Mississippi River on a raft and exploring caves. My parents never talked to me about what I really wanted to do with my life in the real world. Black parents have a need to show concern for the future of their children. God gives us children, and it don't matter whether they are adopted, stepchildren, or biological children. It is your responsibility to see that your child receive every possible chance to become successful. No one will give them anything in the real world, and it's a known fact that there are more people at the bottom of the pile than there are on the top of the pile.

Anyone can be a failure without much effort, but it takes a very determined, hardworking person to succeed at any level. Education is the key to calling your own shots and setting yourself apart from everyone else. Black parents must remember that all good things concerning our children comes from our heavenly Father and that none of us can do anything on our own. We must teach our children, making them understand the importance of developing a trusting relationship with God. Teach them to love all people in this world, regardless of sex, color, or creed. Know what is best for your children and never give up on a seemingly impossible feat of rearing a child correctly. When a parent feels like giving up, show the child love even more. "Herein is our love made perfect." (John 4:17) It's that perfect (complete) love which will create a bond between you and the problem child.

Black children need to know that they are second to no one. They need to know that they are someone special because God doesn't make any junk. We need to make our children feel good about being black Americans. I remember when I was in high school we did not have black history. I remember that we did have one chapter on slavery. I felt embarrassed about such a topic with white children in the same classroom. We need to make our children feel good about black history and culture. There are just too many negative images of black people on television and in the newspaper. It is quite a task for two parents to rear a child. Consequently, a single parent has even less of a chance to be an adequate parent.

Inner city parents have to deal with black on black crime, drugs, gangs, and low-paying jobs. These are social problems. Black children without proper training from their parents are the ones who do not see their way out of the inner city. Police cars are always present. Drugs are being used and sold in broad daylight. Those are the wayward black youth who don't have any respect for anyone, not even their own parents. There are too many unregistered guns on the streets of the inner city to keep children safe. Black parents are in dire need of teaching their children to first love themselves by giving them a sense of belonging. Let them know that they are important to you and encourage them to learn about world history, which encompasses black history. By teaching them world history, they will learn that there was no such continent as Europe and that Africa was the beginning of civilization. By teaching them world history, they will learn what motivated the Europeans to steal the land that was already occupied by the Indians, steal the Africans from their land, and bring them to this country. They will learn how their languages and some cultures were left across the Atlantic Ocean. So, let them know how important the sacrifices of their ancestors were in building the country in which they now live. Please encourage them to learn about their history so that they will learn who they are. *Those who forget their past are condemned to relive it. (Unknown)*

Blacks were called the "N" word which was – and still is – a very disrespectful word to call anyone. Then we were labeled Negroes. Even though Negro sounded better, it was close to the "N" word. Now, the "N" word is accepted by some when it is pronounced a certain way. In the "60's we called ourselves Negroes. This was cool. In the 70's we were called blacks. From the 90's until now, we are referred to as African Americans. What I cannot understand is why we just can't all be Americans – period? Black people are here to stay, like it or not. It doesn't seem as though we are going anywhere any time soon. So why not just get along as one Nation under God. Why not?

Black parents do not have to allow their children to be consumed by the inner city streets. They could try to create some type of trust between themselves and their children so that they will feel comfortable enough to talk to them whenever they are having problems. Sometimes my boys say that I am tripping whenever I don't agree with them. I realize that there is a large generation gap between us, but I don't give in when I know that my decision is for their own good. Today young people are much smarter than we were at their age. Therefore, we have got to be that much smarter than our parents were at our age. Today youth will try us in any way possible in order to get us to see things their way. That is why we as parents have got to stand firm by the decisions we make and, at the same time, let our children understand that they are children and we are the parents!

If you have a child on drugs or alcohol, then seek professional care as soon as possible. Some things we as parents cannot fix on our own no matter how hard we try. There are a great number of black kids who are out of control and a great number of parents who do not know what to do in order to bring them under control. We have a responsibility to our children to rear them to be both respectful and productive. The reason for the rash of school shootings is because we are failing as parents. We pretend not to know that the blood of those innocent children is on the hands of all parents – black and white.

It is time for parents to realize that when we allowed politicians to remove prayer from the schools of our children, we were also removing the greatest protection known to mankind. God is not pleased with the schools removing prayers. Thessalonians II 3:2 Paul tells us, "Pray too, that we will be saved out of the clutches of evil men, for not everyone loves the Lord." God loves our children very much, but He wants us to show love toward Him also, even in our schools. Without God's protection the devil has a chance to steal the lives of our children in classrooms throughout America. Black America cannot improve our way of living without love and protection from God. Our children live by the examples of their parents, and as parents we must live by the example of Jesus Christ. I believe that all of the problems do not lay with our children, but stem from us parents. Many black parents, as well as many white parents, are failing to teach their children the word of God.

How can we contend that we love our children when we don't provide them with the tools they need to survive in this world? Let's face it. Some of us show more love toward our pets than we show toward our children. We even go as far as to refer to our pets as our children. Meanwhile, our children are out doing whatever they want to do without parental supervision. It is not love when parents support their kids by selling drugs. It is not love when parents lie to keep their children out of trouble by saying that their child was at home all night when he or she was really out breaking the law. It is not helping your child at all to cover up for his or her wrongdoings.

When I was a young lad growing up, I respected my elders because I had no choice in the matter. Back then we received an old fashioned whipping from every parent in the neighborhood; and when my mother found out, I'd receive another butt whipping . Today if you dare tell someone's child anything for his or her own good, you can almost count on his or her mother and/or father to knock on your door to confront you about their child.

I want to share with you what my friend, Daryl Gaddis from New Orleans, shared with me through the internet. People over 30 and the rest who need to know! People over 30 should be dead. According to today's regulators and bureaucrats, those of us who were kids in the 40's, 50's, 60's, or even maybe the early 70's probably shouldn't have survived. Our baby cribs were covered with bright colored lead-based paint. There was nothing to stop us from sticking a fork in an electrical outlet.

We had no childproof lids on medicine bottles, doors, or cabinets. When we rode our bikes, we had no helmets. Teenage hitchhiking was normal, as children we would ride in cars with no seat belts or air bags. Riding in the back of a pickup truck on a warm day was always a special treat.

We drank water from the garden hose and not from a bottle. We ate cupcakes, bread and butter, and drank soda pop with sugar in it. However, we never became overweight because we were always outside playing. We shared one soft drink with four friends. From this one bottle, no one actually died. We would spend hours building go carts out of scraps and would ride them down the hill only to find out we forgot the brakes. After running into the bushes a few times, we learned to solve the problem.

We would leave home in the morning and play all day long as long as we were home when the street lights came on. No one was able to reach us by cell phones because there were none. Unthinkable! We did not have Play Stations, Nintendo 64. X-Boxes, or any other video games. Neither did we have cable, video movies, surround sound, personal computers, nor internet chat rooms. We had friends! We went out and found them. We played ball, and sometimes the ball would hurt. We fell out of trees, got cuts, broke bones, and knocked out teeth; and there were no lawsuits from these accidents and no one was blamed but us.

Remember accidents? We had fights, punched each other, and got black and blue. So, we learned to get over it or punch harder the next time. We made up games with sticks and tennis balls. We ate worms, and made mud pies. Regardless of what we were told would happen to us, we did not put out any eyes, nor did the worms live inside us forever. We rode bikes or walked to a friend's home, knocked on the door or rang the doorbell. Sometimes we just walked in to talk to them. Little league had tryouts, but not everyone made the team. Those who didn't make the team went out and started their own team. Some students chose not to be as smart as others. So, they failed a grade and were held back to repeat the same grade.

The ideal of a parent bailing us out of jail when we broke the law was unheard of. They actually sided with the law, imagine that! This generation has produced some of the best risk takers, problem solvers, and inventors. The past fifty years have been an explosion of innovation and new ideals. We have freedom, failure, success, and responsibility. We learned how to deal with it all, and you are one of them Congratulations! Please pass this on to others who have had the blessing of growing up into adults before lawyers and government regulated our lives "for our own good". It kind of makes you want to run through the house with scissors, doesn't it?

Before Hillary Clinton was even born, someone said "It takes a whole tribe to raise a child." Many heard Mrs. Clinton make this statement, but it has been around – at least in the black community – for quite some time. Mrs. Clinton was implying that we all must be involved in the upbringing of each one's children. It's a very simple theory, and it is a proven one because the theory really works. Black parents must become a tribe as we once were, depending upon each other in the rearing of our children.

We have a need to address the drug problems that is overcoming the black youth across this country. We have a need to become a tribe in order to save our children and our dying race. It is time for black parents to let our children know that we love them and will not expect anything less than their best behavior. Some black parents have a need for a new beginning and a fresh start. We need not concentrate on status quo as much as we need to concentrate on what needs to be done about the problems right now. Get solutions that bring results.

If some black parents do not make a change, then black children will surely continue to drop out of school. Nothing will change unless black parents are willing to make a change for the better. Success for our children begins with their parents. Being black has nothing to do with success or failure. Parents have everything to do with how their child turns out in life. Everyone has a choice. When you make the right decisions, only then will you become successful in life. It's lonely at the top, so take someone with you. I hope that we do a better job with rearing our children because if we don't, there won't be a black America to contend with at all.

Some black parents don't seem to be overly concerned about the future of the black youth. Before we can overcome the stumbling blocks in which we have placed in front of our youth, we will first have to be willing to set better examples for our children. There are just too many undisciplined black youth out in the street. We are heading toward losing several generations of children simply because we are unwilling to accept the fact that we have lost control of our children. Young black parents want to become friends with their children instead of a parent. It's all right to be friendly to your children, but being a good parent and role model is more important.

CHAPTER FOUR

BLACK WOMEN

"For God has brought you with a great price. So, use every part of your body to give back to God because He owns it." (I Corinthians 6:20) Many black women need to seek some type of reassurance from God concerning rearing their children. If God isn't a part of your life, then nothing will go according to your plan. Black women must use what they have in whatever way it takes to please God. If black women would honor God, then He will remember them and their children.

Black women are more and more becoming the heads of their households in America because black men have become, for the most part, shiftless and lacking in resources needed to care for their families. Needless to say, black women have joined the working class of America. Black women are vastly becoming both father and mother for their children because of the loss of morals of black men.

Our women are placed in an unfamiliar position of being the bread winners for their families. In many cases these same black women are forced to choose between welfare and accepting a low-paying job in order to simply make ends meet.

Black women often choose desperate measures for their intense situations because they are left to fend for themselves and their children without the aid of a husband or father to help them out. My sister-in-law, Barbara Carter, has sent three daughters to college. Her fourth daughter is starting as a freshman in a state university. Two daughters now have degrees. One is an attorney at law in Baton Rouge, Louisiana. I wanted to mention this because Barbara is a single mother of four. It was not at all easy for her, but she overcame being a mother on welfare. She has set examples for her girls so that they will not depend on the system to take care of them.

These strong, black women seem to summon an inner strength through desire. However, they can't put desire on a plate in order to feed their children. Most black women have always displayed courage and leadership. Harriet Tubman organized the Underground Railroad to help lead many slaves to freedom. Several black Americans don't like hearing the truth, but I promised the truth from the very start. So, here it goes again: The Underground Railroad would not have been successful without the many white families risking their lives by providing shelter for runaway slaves to hide. White Americans hid slaves in their basements, cellars, and barns. It took a tremendous amount of courage for Ms. Tubman to retrieve slaves from plantations and guide them to freedom. Moreover, it could not have been done without the help of white people. Not all whites owned slaves, and not all whites supported the institution of slavery.

Harriet Tubman took on this great task time after time without regard for her own safety or life. Black men even depended upon her to save them from captivity. The bottom line is that a black man instead of a black woman should have volunteered for this endeavor in the first place! Even today black men depend heavily upon the black woman to be an equalizer for the black man's not being responsible. Black women have more humility than the black man when it comes to their pride.

Rosa Parks of Atlanta, Georgia is another example of the liberal black woman. Ms. Parks is the mother of the civil rights movement for her people; a black woman who refused to give up her seat on the city bus to a white person, displayed intestinal fortitude. Because of the actions of Ms. Parks, a massive boycott of city buses took place. Today black men, black women, and black children have the right to sit anywhere they please on any city bus throughout the United States. Once again, where was the courage of the black man? It took a frail, black woman to achieve what should have been challenged by a black man.

Black women still today are taking their places in this country without reservation. Black women have become the strength of the black race, and it's only a matter of time before these great women move to the forefront of the black man. Most mothers are closer than the fathers are to their children and more loved by them because they are always there for them. Many black fathers only want bragging rights and not the responsibility of caring for their children. For every black father who provides for his children, there are at least three who could care less. As for those who don't seem to care, the burden is left with the black, single mother.

More truth: Black women have been abused in America for more than four centuries. They are the first to tell you that they're not taking it anymore. Black women were bred like cattle during slavery and raped by white slave owners. Black slaves also raped black women. After all, who were the black women going to tell? Whenever their master or overseers sent a black stud to breed with a black woman, most of the time it was rape. No one back then needed the blessing of the black slave woman to mate with her. This would be considered rape today. These ungodly men would do the same to black girls as young as 10 or 11 years of age without the permission of their masters. The same black men were beaten and treated like caged animals. This fact of history is still the mentality of today's black men. They don't have any respect for black women or girls. Young, black girls are sought out by black men even more today. Oftentimes, these girls agree to these forbidden relationships. In doing so, they grow up to be scarred, black women with low self-esteem. These same young, black women become dependent upon men for the rest of their lives. They place their trust in men who don't hang around until a child is conceived. From this time on, love is not part of the relationship.

That is a big part of the reason why so many black children come from single-parent homes. This cycle starts over with the single parent child. Ninety-five percent of single, black parents are women because the father has abandoned his family. A black father can come and go at will, but a black mother has no way out. So, they stay with their children. Some mothers will even give their children away to someone, even to the fathers who can't take care of themselves. Many black women have to depend upon stepfathers or boyfriends to support their children. There are good, black fathers out there. However, the number of single, black mothers is growing by the day. If it were not for black women being there for their children, it would be even more problems with the black youth. The number of troubled, black youth would be staggering and more than society could contend with.

Black women deserve much more than black men are willing to give them. Truth: The white race has more respect for black women than they do for black men. Afro American women are basically playing a tremendous part in keeping black America afloat. It is high time for these women to step forward and lead black America out of self-bondage. The black man seems to grow weaker as the black woman grows stronger and wiser by the day. We are starting to lose our women to other races of men simply because there are so few successful black men available. So many black men are no longer willing to be the breadwinners for our families. Our women not only bring home the bacon, but they cook it too.

Several black men tend to abandon their children at a very young age or not claim them at all. Our children are now calling their grandparents "Mom" and "Dad" because many of them are reared by their grandparents. Black grandparents play a major role in supporting their single, black daughters and their grandchildren. They maintain peace at family gatherings and hold our families together at the same time. These Ebony senior citizens are taking the responsibilities of the once active black father.

Thank God for black grandparents and for their wisdom. Our black children would be even more out of control if not for the love and support of their grandparents.

A black woman's best asset is her trust in God. Her belief and fear of God is the sole reason why she is able to provide for her children. The black church provides little or no shelter in the midst of the storm for black, single mothers. Black churches do not venture outside of its Godly confines in order to help our race. I am saying these things about our churches in hopes that Christians can understand the importance of helping outside of the church. Here is some more truth: There are ways outside the church to save souls. I mean that the only way for black women to benefit from a black church is to go in and hear the word of God. I must admit that black churches do provide God's word but not much of anything else. There are not many of our churches that show concern for the many battered black women who need help. There is more work to be done outside of the church than there is inside. I hate to seem as though I am bashing our black churches, but I believe that any institution that is in a position to provide a service toward uplifting their people must do so. It's not about money. It's about reaching out in love to those who may need a hand.

Black women may play a small role in the church; but no matter how small the part, they are loyal to their church and pastor. We are told to pay tithes of 10 percent of our earnings to God, and I personally believe that is the right thing to do. I often wonder what is being done for single, black mothers; or are these women a priority in the black church? It is the duty of the church to render aid to those in need. We have a need to implement programs within the church in order to help build self-esteem in young black mothers and, in return, they will become better mothers.

Black women are a minority. The odds are very much against them, but I believe that they will rise to whatever challenge that they may encounter. Black women have suffered in the past years, but they have survived with dignity. They have been relentless in their pursuit of being a valuable asset to our race as well as displaying graciousness. These women have been outwardly abused by the black man and misunderstood by the white man. Racism has played a role in the oppression of black women, but being disrespected by black men is what plunged the fatal dagger of disparity into their hearts. Black women are on the rise in America. They are steadily becoming a mainstay in corporate America, entertainment, and even politics. Black women are definitely a force to be reckoned with in this nation.

Black women are now receiving more education than black men and are working for more prominent companies than ever before. Still black women need support from within their race and fair treatment from black men. I applaud black mothers in this country for their willingness to give of themselves for the sake of their children and race. There are many black women who are out working and are not receiving a handout from taxpayers. Those are the women in whom I am referring to. Also, single women who don't have any choice but to receive assistance because their jobs don't pay enough for them to provide for their children are still trying. I pray that black women will receive the recognition in which they truly and justly deserve for their perseverance.

God decided that it was not good for man to be alone, and He made a companion for Adam to suit his every need. The Lord put Adam to sleep and took one of his ribs then made it into a woman. Still today men treat women like they're one of their ribs. Women are a gift from God in which he gave man to become his wife and bear his children. Black men cannot continue to abuse the blessing that God has bestowed upon him. God intended for men to love their wives and take care of their children. I truly believe that God is sorry that He made any of us. God said, "I will blot out from the face of the earth all mankind that I created. Yes, and the animals too, and the reptiles, and the birds. For I am sorry I made them." (Genesis 6:7) I believe that God did not intend for black women or any women, regardless of color, to suffer by the hands of man. It is not the will of God for the children to be fatherless or poor. We can only blame ourselves for not rearing our children according to the word of God. Being a parent is also a gift from our Creator, and He expects for us to sow good seeds. If we sow seeds of righteousness, then we as parents reap crops of love and salvation for our children.

I say to all men "Love your wives as God loves you. Respect her as you would want to be respected by others. Be a man and work hard as your father did to make sure that you did not have to suffer. I can safely say that it does not please God for a man to run out on his responsibilities to his wife and children. For whatsoever a man sow, he shall also reap. Mankind has disappointed God for leaving so many children to suffer, and these same children will become the same way their fathers were to them. Any man can be a father, but any father can't be a man unless he owns up to his responsibilities toward his family

CHAPTER FIVE

SUCCESSFUL BLACK MEN

How does a man become wise? The first step is to trust and reverence the Lord. (Proverbs 1:7).

Some of us seem to forget our hardships when we are no longer in the rat race. We tend to forget the struggle in which we endured in order to become successful. We no longer remember those who struggled along the way to the top but did not make it. Some successful black men are guilty of this sudden loss of memory. There are those few who do all within his power to lend some knowledge, but it's not easy to pull the black man out of his oppression.

Another truth: Successful white men are the backbone of their race, and I honestly respect them for their leadership within their race. Successful white men will pull another white man up with him without reservation, but black men are afraid that someone will replace them. Some blacks won't even tell another black whenever there is an opening at his place of employment. As I go on, I will expose a few of our well-known successful black men and give credit to those who deserve our respect.

When things don't go right for us at times, we are very quick to yell out racial discrimination. Truth: Black men will discriminate against each other even more so than the white will. Some blacks use each other for their own personal gains with no remorse whatsoever. Here's a perfect example of the truth in which I promised to you right from the very start:

Mr. Tank Black is a very successful sports agent for professional football players in the NFL and has been for 21 years. So it's safe to say that Mr. Black is a successful black man, to say the least. However, Tank Black is being charged with giving substantial amounts of money to collegiate football players and also buying expensive cars for them. All of this was done in order to persuade these young black men to sign with his firm whenever they enter the NFL. Now all of Mr. Tank's actions are illegal and not authorized by the NFL or the NCAA.

Mr. Black cares nothing about the long-term welfare of those young men. He is only concerned about his own personal gain. It gets even worse as we continue. Tank faced suspension from dealing with the NFL by the commissioner, who was Gene Upshaw (former Oakland Raider). Mr. Upshaw is also a successful black man and well-respected. Criminal and federal charges are pending against Mr. Black for prematurely dealing with three black collegiate football players. Thanks to Mr. Black, these three young men have placed their college careers in jeopardy.

So what does Tank do? He does what seems to always work: he files a racial discrimination suit. How far are we willing to go in order to justify our actions? When are we going to stop pointing fingers in the direction of others in times of trouble? Tank Black cares nothing about being a role model for young, black men. He is not the type of man in whom anyone would want his or her sons to pattern after. Truth: How can Mr. Black file a racial discrimination suit against the NFL when all parties involved are black? Now how low can Mr. Black go?

Do not misunderstand me. I realize that there are times when a discrimination suit is appropriate and should be filed because black people are not always treated fairly due to their skin color; and that is, by no means, right. However, we should never use our skin color as an excuse for failure or a way out of trouble. Discrimination suits are for rectifying a wrong done to any person because of his or her color, sex, or religion. We as black people sometimes pull the race card for the wrong reasons. No man has the right to discriminate against another man, but nevertheless, it is not right to use discrimination as a weapon.

Let's move on to the NAACP because Tank Black is a bit too much for his own good. The National Association for the Advancement of Colored People. I would like to know who the colored people are who they represent. There are a great number of poor, black people who have never met a NAACP member knowingly or has never been formerly invited to one of their meetings. This organization is headed by – you guessed it – successful, black men who could care less about poor, blacks. I refuse to even compromise the truth in any form. Most poor blacks don't even know what the letters N-A-A-C-P stand for. If you don't believe it to be a fact, then go out and ask 10 inner city children. I understand that the NAACP can't help every single black person in need. They are mostly known for high profile cases. What about the poor blacks who need help the most? Truth: Successful, black men did not get where they are by dealing with the problems of the poor, black people.

Black Americans are not being treated equally in several of the NAACP cases, and that will never change. Black people must change the way we treat each other. We've got to work together and share the load of regression. The successful, black man must work with the poor, black man before any of us can ever begin to progress an inch. I realize that all white people are not good people, just as not all black people are good people.

Blacks cannot control prejudice, but we can control how we think about prejudice people with the help of God. Just as black Americans don't like to be called the "N" word, the whites don't like to be called "honkey" or "crackers". You see that all people deserve respect and should be treated like you want to be treated. For every prejudice person, there are two who are not judging others by the color of their skin. There are a lot of good people in this world who do not understand racism and don't want to be a part of its destruction. Truth: Everyone is not out to get black America, and everyone doesn't want to see us suffer.

Until President Barack Obama was elected president, the black race had been without leadership since the death of Dr. Martin Luther King, Jr. Many people consider Jesse Jackson to be a successful, black man; but I know him to be very successful at fooling black Americans by telling them just what they want to hear. Truth: Mr. Jackson is not the leader that Dr. King was and never will be. Rev. Jackson has made more gains for himself and America than he has for black America. What I mean is that he has not stepped forward as a black leader. What we don't need is another black politician who is seeking selfish, personal acknowledgments and gains.

President Bill Clinton has done more for black people than any so-called black leaders and their organizations have done in the past thirty-five years. The majority of the black race has looked to former President Clinton for leadership and solutions in the past. Some blacks refer to President Clinton as the first black president because he committed his oval office to a better America for black Americans. Many of us are a lost people in the sense that we don't know how to solve our own problems within our race. Many blacks struggling because we haven't learned how to solve our problems without help from the white race.

There is a need for successful, black men from all professional walks of life to come together and create solutions in order to organize the structure of the black race. Truth: We need black men to be men and take a stand for the progression of black America on behalf of our youth. We cannot continue to hide behind the dress tails of Rosa Parks and Harriet Tubman. We as black men must first overcome our inner souls by overcoming our black way of thinking. We cannot begin to solve our problems unless we realize that there is a problem within many of us. There are more than enough qualified, successful black men to organize a plan of action that would make a positive difference for black Americans.

The *Bible* says the truth will make you free indeed. So, I must continue to provide you with the truth according to the word of God. Now let's take a serious look at the famous Million Man March for what it was really worth. The Muslim religion organized this big march that no one profited from but the airlines, gas stations, and Greyhound buses. Nothing changed except the crime rate the day of the march. Crime was at an all-time low in the black neighborhoods because so many brothers were in Washington D.C. I am not being sarcastic. I am only pointing out the good or lack thereof that came out that march for black men.

The Muslim religion would indeed be the most powerful and spiritual religion on earth today if they would only accept our Lord and Savior Jesus Christ as the son of God. They believe Him to be only a prophet. Jesus was not only a prophet, but the Son of Jehovah, the almighty God. In Matthew 16:16 Simon Peter (Jesus' disciple) said to Jesus, "Thou art the Christ, the Son of the living God." The word "prophet" in the *Random House College Dictionary* means a man called by God to be one of His own. Jesus has to be held higher than a prophet because He is the true Son of God, period. Don't get me wrong, for I have great respect for the intentions of the Muslim religion just as I do for all other religions. However, I will never agree with their belief of who Jesus is. If God said it to be true, then I believe it to be true. That's all I've got to say about that.

Louis Farrakhan is a whole other issue by himself. Farrakhan is a black, Muslim; but I personally refuse to accept him as a black leader or an advocate of black ideals. Farrakhan's ideals are very harmful to the progression of the black race. He is for a new, black nation that does not include white people. That is not any more possible than for whites to create a nation without blacks. Truth: Are blacks better than the KKK? We have got to believe that all people are created equal and that only God can judge us. Black America must create a new nation within our race with respect and regard for all other races of people on the face of this earth. A new black nation must be organized in the sense of abolishing the old, nonproductive ways of the present black America. We have the need to allow a new and better black people to emerge from the ashes of disparity. It will take a determined black people in order to accomplish this feat.

Minister Farrakhan is a very intelligent man, to say the least; but I don't, by any means, want a Civil War. He may not have outright used the term "civil war". However, all of his teaching points in the direction of destruction. Blacks must realize the importance of the word of God as well as education. I must say again that I mean no disrespect toward the Muslim religion. Muslims want pretty much the same things that I want for my people. The Muslims want progression for our race, and so do I. However, I firmly feel that there is a right way to become productive; and there is a wrong way. I am for what is right at this stage of my life. I have not always cared for white people, but during those low phases of my life I really didn't like myself. I blamed white America, but now I realize that I was responsible for how my life was unfolding.

I am not proclaiming to be better than anyone. I am not at all beyond fault, and neither is the Muslim religion without fault concerning the regression of black America. Self-inventory is in order for each black person in a realistic manner. We must, at the same time, be willing to change for the better of all people. I can promise you that I will become a successful, black man because I now realize that I am not in this world for my own purpose. I represent the black race, and my actions reflect upon every black male. You can accept this fact to be true or not.

White people are not blue-eyed devils, and black people don't grow tails at midnight. We are all people, one people under God. I will do all within my power to promote black pride and black education for our youth. Freedom and justice should be for all Americans without reservation or a price. I see every day that many blacks are still being oppressed, but it has always been that way for us. We must learn to move around racism and seek out an education. If we can do that, then I can assure you of a productive turn around.

All races have a responsibility toward crime prevention, and everyone must do his or her part to make it safe to go outside your home. The white race has become somewhat more acceptable toward blacks, and most of them really want to understand our anger. A lot of times we will not allow anyone to get close to us because we have not learned to trust outside of our race. We have a fear of being out of our safety zone. We have a fear that the world is out to get us. We think that being black is being strong and defensive. We will not let our guards down not even for one moment. Well, it's time to let go of the past and work toward progress.

O.J. Simpson was a great running back in the NFL and a successful, black man. The Simpson trial was a very sad era for the progression of black America. It brought about even more separation and strife between blacks and whites in this country. O.J. had always been a good role model. However, it was all taken away from him in his trial. Even though O.J. Was acquitted, he has to live the rest of his life as a guilty man. Truth: Because of the many discrepancies in evidence, the court allowed him to go free. White Americans still believe him to be guilty and still prosecute him today without warrant. O.J. Even lost a civil suit to the parents of the victims. I don't want to believe to this day that The Juice could have possibly committed such an awful crime, but many whites consider him to be guilty.

Black America, on the other hand, prayed for their fallen hero and rejoiced at the verdict of not guilty. Most whites were very disappointed and angry. Truth: The black race pulled together as one for O.J. Simpson. So, why can't we use that same energy toward the progression of our people and solve some of the problems which are plaguing our race? Why can't we have we have that same compassion for each other within the black community? We expected the worst for O.J. At the very same time, we blamed the white man. Instead, we should have learned from that bad experience and simply moved on to our problems at hand. Blacks did not profit one single thing as a race from the Simpson trial. So, why should we have gotten so caught up in something that none of us knew anything about first hand? Only O.J. Simpson knows the truth about where he was at the time of those killings. I'm speaking of both blacks and whites, making pure fools of themselves.

There are many productive, black men in America today; and there is no way that I can mention them all. I realize that I may appear to be anti-black because I choose to be honest about the self-destruction of the black man. I simply refuse to continue to look the other way anymore. I pray that any one thing in this book would put back some of the pride into black America. My goal is not to embarrass black people, but to motivate my people with the truth. We have got to reach the point to whereas we are sick and tired of being last in line for everything. We have got to want more than just happy to be in America. We must want to be a vital part of this great country by becoming more than a member or a citizen.

Mr. Tavis Smiley is a talk show host for Black Entertainment Television (BET). Mr. Smiley is also concerned about crime and drugs within black America. He is very much a successful, black man; and I personal admire his show. However, Mr. Smiley is not generally as open on black America as I am. Most of the time, Tavis takes a more positive approach to the problems we bring on ourselves. He has many successful blacks as guests on his show. Some successful blacks tend to talk about how to become successful and elaborate on what to expect in prosperous America. Some black people will never know how to become successful until we can understand more of what is wrong within our race.

I listened to Tavis Smiley in Atlanta, Georgia on the radio every single morning on the Tom Joyner Morning Show. Tavis knows what it takes to repair black America, but he cannot do it alone. Tom Joyner's Morning Show is also pro-black, and we need more black shows like his.

Hello Ms. Dupree, Sybil, Mr. Joyner and all the morning crew. You give lots of positive messages to black people. -What's up J. Anthony Brown? We like hearing what's right with us, but we don't like it when we hear the truth about where we are going wrong.

There are many talented black men in this nation, and those are the men who can make a positive difference. Most black youth from an early age want to become a professional athlete or some type of entertainer. Black children want to be like Mike (Michael Jordan), but the simple truth is that black youth have a better chance of becoming a doctor or lawyer. Successful black men have a need to educate our children on how to become successful. They need to be told by black doctors, firemen, lawyers, policemen, teachers, mayors, athletes, and parents to stay in school to receive a good education.

There is a great deal of talent within the rap music industry. Tupac and Master P are two of my favorites among many others. I like P. Diddy, 50 Cent, Nelly, and Ja'rue also because all of them are successful, black men, in my opinion. Tupac was killed at the height of his career. He was starting to show a great deal of promise for black, young youth before he was gunned down. Tupac had every element it took to make a difference for black youth. However, we will never know just how far Tupac would have gone.

Master P is in a league all by himself and has no limit as to how far he may want to take his thing. Master P has given new meaning to the term "no limit" and always have the door open to people of his own race. Remember when I said earlier in chapter one that it's all right to help people of your own race as long as you don't hurt anyone by doing so. Master P has a hand in many money-making ventures, but he has not forgotten where he came from. It's all right to remember that you were poor. Use that memory as a determination to achieve a better life for yourself, your family, and your people. It is okay to recall your past life even as a drug addict because if you don't remember the pain, then you can never be free from the drug.

Now, last but certainly not least by any stretch of the imagination, Mr. Don King – yes, Mr. King. He is not a favorite of among many people. However, Mr. King is well-respected by both blacks and whites. He is very successful as a boxing promoter and should be respected. Mr. King is known for his dealings as a promoter of many fights involving black fighters. Here comes more truth without reservation: Don King is accused of being dishonest by some of those same fighters. He has been to federal prison for tax evasion, in which many of us don't report every dime. However, Mr. King's taxes consist of millions of dollars; and that alone draws the attention of the IRS.

Mr. King takes out time from his busy schedule to talk to poor black children about drugs, success, and staying in school. He may not be honest with the federal government, but he still shows concern for black children. Mr. King may not be a perfect role model, but what he does for the poor children is more important than a successful role model who does nothing to better his race. My hat is off to Mr. King, and I don't need a recommendation from him as to where to get my taxes prepared. (Just joking)

Successful, black men have to become role models within the black race for black children. Truth: They have a responsibility to go back to black, inner city areas where they are needed the most. Black professionals have the responsibility to carry the burden of the regression of black people in America. It's not about being successful, black men. It's more to being successful, and at some point we've got to become a man. We've got to take a stand for our children's sake.

CHAPTER SIX

BLACK YOUTH

Children, obey your parents; this is the right thing to do because God has placed them in authority over you. (Ephesians 6:1)

Black youth have the opportunity of becoming the prominent Americans in which most blacks in the previous generations have failed to do. It will not be an easy task to accomplish by any means, but it is not impossible. Today black children are not being prepared to face the world, and that's not being fair to them at all. The world can be a cold place for those youth who are wasting their lives on the streets. The black society is letting down their black children. We are to blame for not rearing our children to be a productive class of young people. America is paying a heavy price for our being so irresponsible in caring for the black youth. Truth: All this country has to offer black youth who drop out of school is the construction of more jail cells to lock them in, and we haven't caught on yet. Truth:

In the next fifty years there will be more homeless blacks than ever before because there are too many black not working toward any type of retirement.

Black parents have the responsibility to prepare their children for the mission of becoming successful adults in America. I must add that there are many parents who are not doing a good job at this time. We are failing in our efforts to reform black youth. We do not always set good examples as parents for our children. It is only right to reward and congratulate our children when he or she does something worthwhile, and we should. What is to be done when we have children who just don't want to do right? These are the children who suffer from low self-esteem. There could be a lack of attention from parents toward that particulars child. We have got to spend time with all of our children, but even more time with the one who needs it most. It pays in the long run to know your children well enough to detect a problem in any one of them before the problem totally consumes your child.

Black parents must learn a way to uplift our youth who are habitual under achievers. Under achieving is caused by low self-esteem. Those are the black youth who will kill themselves or others, do drugs, sell drugs, and drop out of school at a young age. Parents have a need to identify such problems before it is too late to do anything about them. There are thousands upon thousands of black youth who need our help. Black or white, Jesus loves all children. In Matthew 18:3 Jesus said, "Verily I say unto you except ye be converted and become as little children, ye shall not enter into the King of heaven. The black youth are very important to the survival of the black race, and the black parent is equally as important to the survival of the black youth.

If we continue to allow our young people to do as they pleased, then we will never overcome ourselves nor will our race prosper. We seem to always be concerned about the wrong things. Black people must not be overly concerned with racism. I'm speaking of being concerned with the degradation of racism to the point where it becomes self-destruction; destroying all that we have gained since Dr. Martin Luther King. Truth: Yes, we must defend our rights but we've got to do it in a reasonable way. Our real battle is to regain control of the black youth instead of fighting for insignificant rights. Truth: The confederate flag in the states of Mississippi, Georgia, and South Carolina have caused many blacks to become insecure. A flag that signifies the loser of the Civil War has been around for well over a hundred years. This flag should have never been placed on the agenda of the NAACP. We need to address present-day problems that are plaguing our black communities.

Allow me to break all of this down so that you will see a much clearer picture of this nonsense summoned by our NAACP. Truth: Black people have got to realize that a lot blood was shed for that piece of cloth. The confederate flag means a great deal to the families of the soldiers who died in the Civil War for what they truly believed to be right at the time. After all, that is what this country is all about. Those principles are what this nation was built upon in the beginning. We are focused upon how the flag is used today, not the fact that the confederate flag is part of black history. Many blacks died fighting under that same flag, and it does not matter whether the NAACP admits it or not.

Sometimes we violate the rights of other races while protecting what we believe to be our rights. I have learned through trial and error to live and let live because life is so very short. The valuable time the NAACP spends protecting unreasonable rights, such as a flag, we should be dealing with the growing rampage of our black youth. Black America and the NAACP should stop peeping under rocks for petty insults against black people. There is plenty out there to last for the next 100 years. I can attest to the fact that if we look for trouble, we will surely find it under every rock. When you don't attack certain situations, they will simply go away without fanfare.

Truth: Black youth are not always afforded all the benefits in which this nation has to offer. Our children have to become better than other races by way of an education in order to reap some of the riches of this country. The reason that black kids have to be better than other races is because "just as good" in most cases is not good enough. Again, black youth must become more efficient than the rest of the world through education in order to be recognized as any kind of asset in America. Black parents have to invest in computers in their homes for their children. We have got to upgrade our children's way of thinking into the 21st century. We have a need to teach our youth how to deal with racism in a civil manner and not allow its evils to set them back.

CHAPTER SEVEN

BLACK SOCIETY

"For the ways of man are before the eyes of the Lord, and he pondereth His entire goings." (Proverbs 5:21) We also experience prejudice within the black society because black people are not limited to just one color within our race. Truth: Some dark-skinned blacks do not care for lighter-skinned blacks and vice versa. Then there are still other shades of black people such as yellows, reds, browns, and biracial. We are a rainbow of people; but no matter how light our skin color, we are all considered black. Even if only one parent is black and the other is white, we are all considered black. Biracial is not always accepted by many whites. In most cases people who are biracial consider themselves to be black anyway.

Black families are not as close as we once were in the old days. Brothers and sisters don't get along, and the black children are rebelling against their parents. Black male youth speak of respect and don't know the meaning of the word. The black society has to show respect before the black youth can know respect. The black youth have to learn respect before the black youth can earn respect. (Keep it real) The black society has to place value upon our youth and let them know that they are important to their race. Black children are growing up too fast without experiencing a childhood.

The black society has ruined our children with expensive clothes, gold teeth, and $100 tennis shoes, most of which we cannot afford in the first place. Then we have the audacity to rave about what we don't have versus what the whites do have. Low income black youth will do anything in order to keep pace with styles. They will sell drugs, steal, and rob because society says if you don't wear brand names, then you are a buster. Truth: The rich get richer and the poor get poorer because of high-priced fashions at the mall. Eighty percent of black society, who buys high-priced fashions, for their children doesn't have a single dime saved toward their child's education. I'll say it again: The black society has to place a value upon our youth.

Most of our society tends to worry about all the wrong things concerning our children. Black teenage girls are having babies at an alarming rate. Their bodies are starting to mature at the young age of 10 or 11. Some are pregnant at 12 years old, and all we are worrying about is how are we going to keep up with the Jones. We must practice tough love with our children and not let them have the upper hand. Be a parent and not a friend, but we are choosing to be a friend and not a parent. You can be a parent and a friend to your children. However, being a parent must take precedent over being friends with our children.

Black addicted men are robbing, stealing, and killing to support their habit. More black Americans are losing their homes, families, cars, jobs, dignity, and lives because of drug abuse. I am going to continue to tell the truth about black America at all cost. Black homes are being left without husbands, fathers, and any kind of support, leaving many black children living in poverty. At what point will the black society place a value upon our children? I will drive home that point until we realize that our black youth have worth.

The elderly members of the black society are forced to fend for abandoned grandchildren because of drug addiction. AIDS are beginning to take a tremendous toll upon on black America while taxpayers are footing the bill for our drug habits. Why shouldn't white America or hardworking blacks be upset for having part of their earnings allocated on endless drug use? Black America has to somehow become a productive society. We must want to deal with the problems that are stemming from substance abuse within the black race. It's our problem, and we must deal with them ourselves.

Black America needs a black leader who is unafraid to speak the truth about the real problems within our black society. Unlike Jesse Jackson and Al Sharpton who tell black America just what they want to hear in order to continue their free ride, we need a leader who will speak the truth without the fear of political ramifications. I'll tell you the truth and that truth being that the real problem in black America is black America. We are our own worst enemy. The problem is as close as our mirror. Blacks must become allies to black America, and that alone will close the gap between white America and us. We are afraid of change, and we don't want change. However, if we don't accept that a change is needed to progress, then we will forever be left behind the eight ball. We have to at least change how we approach our problems.

Black America must show less hostility toward each other and other races. We must confront our fears and not be such an angry people. We still have time to stop our regression and become the people that we were meant to be. We can be a productive people, but we've got to put God first in our lives and trust Him to guide us out of disparity. The black society can't give in because our youth depend on us. Our survival as a race depends upon our ability to change and not upon our ability to adapt. Blacks have a need to trust each other like we did in the old school days.

Black on black crime is totally out of control, and black parents are becoming afraid of their own children. It has become unsafe both inside and outside your home. An extremely extensive change has to be made with the black society. We are almost at the point of no return, and it's high time that we fight against crime in our society. If blacks would pull together, then we would be able to overcome whatever there is for us to overcome. Truth: We have got to understand that one of the major problems that black people have is other black people.

A large percentage of black society is responsible for all of the setbacks we have endured. Now we have got to learn just how we can make it right as a people. We can no longer sit on our hands and expect others to do things for us. The white society has a great deal more respect for black women than they do black men. Afro American women are basically carrying the black race as far as being respected by others outside the race. The black society has a need for more of these women to step forward and help lead us out of self-bondage. As black men grow weaker from his black way of thinking, black women are growing stronger. We are starting to see more black women with white men because there are fewer productive black men available.

Truth: The Department of Corrections only harvests bigger and better criminals. While incarcerated, inmates learn how not to get caught from the other inmates' mistakes that lead them to get arrested in the first place.

At the same time inmates improve upon their criminal techniques. The only prisoners who become rehabilitated are the ones who are truly sorry for their crimes and have assumed responsibility for his or her actions. It is my belief that the prison system and parole board have failed miserably because three out of five inmates return to prison or jail after committing yet another crime. I'm merely pointing out yet another failure of the Department of Corrections and how those very same failures are affecting the black society as a whole.

Prisons are very much needed. However, there has to be more control and more education. Here are some fast facts that may interest you about our prison system. Seventy percent of all crimes are directly or indirectly drug-related. Believe it or not, 90 percent of all female inmates are involved in homosexual activity, and 35 percent of male inmates are involved in same sex affairs. About 35 to 40 percent of all inmates cannot read or cannot comprehend what they can barely read. I am sure that prisons are doing the best that they can with why they have, but maybe the current system is not designed to make better people out of inmates. After all, we can only get out of the prison system what we put into the prison system. Maybe there is someone who does not intend for prisoners to get out and stay out. It could be that someone believes that the American society is better off with our prisoners full. In fact, many believe that the more prison population goes up, the more crime goes down.

The black society must deal with street level drug users and drug dealers in order to help prevent the overcrowding of our nation's prison system. Overcrowding only adds to the many burdens of the prison system, and we need to reach out to drug users before they reach prisons. Drug usage and drug dealing have the entire black society in bondage, and we seem not to notice at all. Black America tends not to want to face the demons (drugs) that are destroying our society and killing our youth. We are sending our children to prison by not doing something about the drug problems they're faced with daily.

There is a great deal of worthwhile anti drug programs available. The black society has to find a way to treat drug addiction. In order to help control crime, we must first control drug usage by focusing upon addiction. Drug usage leads to crime, and crime leads to prison. It's just that simple. If we can slow down usage, then we can slow down crime. You don't need a master's degree to figure any of this out. All you need is common sense.

The black society has become adapted to expecting the worst instead of working toward what is better. We blame the police, the white man, and even the government for the problems in which we refuse to acknowledge to ourselves. We will acknowledge our problems to everyone by complaining but not by applying any efforts to mend them. We want help from others, but we don't want to shoulder any of the blame. It's like saying, I dropped the vase but the floor broke it instead, of saying that I dropped the vase and broke it due to my carelessness. If we would learn to accept responsibility for our actions, then we will be able to confront our problems on our own.

Truth: I broke the law, I used drugs, I put myself in prison, and I'm very sorry for what I put so many innocent people through, including my own family. I've assumed responsibility for my own actions against others and feel good about what I've become today. It's easy for me to say, "I'm sorry. Excuse me. I love you," and many other good things, but until I live what I say, it won't mean a thing. I like myself today, and in liking myself it's a giant step toward loving myself. I have no concerns as to what tomorrow might bring. I can only live for today and pray that I can be a blessing to someone during the course of today. All of my downfalls began with me and proceeded under my own freewill. I can't blame anyone but myself, and I won't blame anyone but myself. I've learned to not trust my own judgment anymore. I depend upon God to guide me trough each awaking day.

The black society must live by the principles of being accountable for our wrongdoings. We have been addicted to failure for far too long. It is not the will of God for black people or any other people to suffer. We bring failure upon ourselves by accepting failure as a part of life. My hopes are that the truth will somehow make a difference for the black society and not be just wishful thinking. We have need of a jump start toward becoming a functional and fundamental society. Truth: Black power will only be achieved through black education.

It has come to the point of not trusting our own judgment and learning to depend on God. I did not say for you to depend upon your church. I will say it again. Depend on God! All the ways of a man are clean in his own eyes, but the Lord weigheth the spirits. (Proverbs 16:2). Not all churches are clean before God's eyes but are only clean to its members and pastors. I can tell you that only God represents the whole truth. Only God can give you a positive and hopeful outlook. As for our black society, we are in need of a spiritual awakening. We must have faith in Jesus Christ along with good works.

If the black society has to fail, we do not have to fail because we're black. We have got to be in control of the outcome of our own future in this nation by becoming responsible for our choices. Our youths' lives depend upon the decisions we make as a society. We are misleading our children and, even worse, we allow our so-called black leaders to poison their young minds. Truth: Jesse Jackson is a prime example of corruption of the black youth, and I won't back down from what I say. We as a society are losing much-needed ground toward becoming a healthy race because of the selfish misrepresentation by Rev. Jackson. I will not tell you what you want to hear in order to win you over, and I will not lie to you in order to be your friend.

I will end this chapter with some of what Shepherd Smith, the founder and president of the Institute for Youth Development, had to say about Jesse Jackson. "We can't have parents, teachers, clergy, and coaches teaching children that violence is unacceptable while role models such as Jesse Jackson's decision to question the expulsions of six black male students in Decatur, Illinois for fighting in the bleachers at a football game. Jesse Jackson publicly teaches them that, "there are no absolute standards for behavior. Everything is relative, and there's and if and but for every transgression."

Real life doesn't work like that, and the sooner Jesse Jackson realizes that, the better off Decatur, Illinois and the rest of America will be. With negative consequences leading to bad behavior, positive learning experiences can never be. There's something wrong here! Wrong lessons, mixed messages, and inappropriate focus on children and violence. For all this we have Jesse Jackson to thank. Perhaps this Thanksgiving I should be thankful that Jesse Jackson is not coming to my children's school district. I can't begin to understand why blacks can't see through Jesse Jackson for what he really represents, which is himself and his family. Rev. Jackson is a publicity seeker and will do anything to be noticed.

Truth: The black society will indeed remain a lost society with leaders like Rev. Jackson and Rev. Sharpton batting for us. Black America will not get to first base with those two as managers of our society. Our youth are becoming more and more confused, and we can't seem to grasp on to just what we are doing to hurt them. Our only hope to become a productive black society is to refrain from being misled by what sounds good from undeserving and unsolicited black leadership. Mr. Shepherd Smith, I am black, and I hear you loud and clear! Thank you.

CHAPTER EIGHT

THE BLACK FAMILY

"There is no condemnation now for those who live in union with Christ Jesus."

(Romans 8:1)

Black families must renew our faith in Christ. Again, black families must renew our faith in Christ. This is very important to the spiritual well-being of the black family and very essential to the survival of the black race. It is impossible to have a healthy family relationship within the black family structure without regard to the word of God. Jesus must be made head of the entire household within the family circle. Black families or any family has to place God over all affairs concerning that family as was done in the past. The black family must hold God true to His word and cash in on His promise to set the captives free. In Micah 7:8 it says, "Our enemies have no reason to gloat over us. We have fallen, but we will rise again. We are in darkness now, but the Lord will give us light". Think about that scripture.

God has not forsaken the black family. Truth: The black family has forsaken God! Black husbands and fathers seem not to want to permit God to be a part of their efforts to rear their children unlike our fathers before us. Black mothers of yesteryear knew the importance of praying in order to keep the family unit strong in Christ. Many black women during those hard times of the past gathered their much-needed strength from praying night and day.

My wife is a woman of God, and I thank God for making her a part of my life. Doris has always been God's anointed strength in our family. Sometimes I wonder if she's aware of just how much influence she has on her family. She worked and cared for three boys – well, four counting myself. At times during my addiction I would be gone for days at a time, getting high with other black fathers and husbands while Doris had to maintain what was left of our black shattered family. I asked her to leave me because I felt that my family would be better off without me. Doris refused to allow me to kill myself and not live up to my God-given responsibility of providing a reasonable living for my family.

Doris never wavered during my drug addiction and stood by my side as if she knew that her prayers for me would be answered. She believed in God's love for me when I didn't believe in myself. She stood steadfast when I took the easy way out by giving up. Doris knew that God had a purpose for my life even when my life seemed hopeless to others. My family suffered a great deal, but with the love of God she held us together. I thank God for Doris because I truly believe that she is my angel in the flesh when I need her most. Doris held us together with the help of God, and I thank them both for giving me hope. I stopped feeling sorry for myself and realized that I was not the only one who was hurting. I hurt my family also.

If I hadn't changed my life of addiction, then I wouldn't be of any use to anyone. With the help of God and the prayers of Doris, I made a change for the better. I regained my life, and I became a supporter of my family once again. I am as free of drugs today as I was yesterday, and I have developed a keen sense of what I want out of life now. I realize that I am not the only one who matters. I now realize that I can't hurt myself without hurting my family. It is impossible to fail myself without failing my family also. I can't love anyone unless I first love myself, and I can't help anyone until I began to love me. I thank God for each and every day no matter what the day may bring. I can't worry about tomorrow or yesterday, but deal only with today on today's terms. If I do this, I'll do just fine. God is my support system because I cannot go it alone.

Many black families seem to believe that everyone outside our race is against them. However, we haven't anyone or anything to fear other than ourselves and our lack of family values. Truth: What we teach our children at home will determine the outcome of their young lives 80 percent of the time. Values within the family begin at home, and it's important as to what examples we set in the family environment for our children. As the old saying goes, "like father like son" and "chip off the old block." Truth: Most bad habits by our black youth are learned within the black household from black parents. Now here we go again, most bad habits learned by our children come from within their own households.

There's also a positive side as to what children learn from their parents, such as having an education, working a steady job, going to church, and being responsible. We are beginning to lose our values, such as eating together as a family. We all eat meals at different times. One may eat at 5:00 pm., while another will eat at 6:00 pm.. Some don't come home and eat at all. We do not sit at the dinner table and discuss the events of the day with our children. Most black families are nothing like the Cosbys, but more like the Adams family. I mean the way most of the blacks live as a family is unreal and unsuitable for prime time television.

Black families are faced with brothers and sisters having different fathers. While one father may support the sister, the brother may not ever see his father at all. This is not at all a healthy way to rear children, but it is the norm for about 50 percent of black families. When you think of a family you may think of a father, a mother, a sister, and a brother. However, that's not the case for many black families. Black women have to seek help outside the family structure to meet the needs of herself and her children, thus, creating different fathers for her children.

Here comes that old truth again: Black women have to look toward other black women for comfort, compassion, and companionship more than ever before. It is a known fact that more and more black women are vastly becoming bisexuals, and a small part of the reason is because more black women are being sentenced to prison that ever before. The main reason is because black men are not there to meet their needs in a long term relationship, and black men are not representing the truth with our women. These are just a few reasons of what breaks up the black family unit.

Truth: Black youth need the firm, but loving, instructions of both parents. Learning is a big part of growing up, and it has to come from both parents under one roof. "Here ye children the instruction of a father, and attend to know understanding." (Proverbs 4:1) Whenever a black family is without a father, then the understanding of Proverbs 4:1 by a father will not be there. The father should be the head of his family. A mother provides love, understanding guidance, peace, and protection from fear. However, God calls upon a father to render support, guidance, spirituality, independence, wisdom, and love. These qualities are what make up a happy family and brings about productive children. When there is no father within the family circle, then the mother must become both a mother and father. Black fathers are needed in order to have a decent chance to become a real family.

The black family must become a more productive unit by having both parents there for support. Parents have got to be more concerned about their child's activities. Let's face it, parents have to know that it's a problem developing when their children are having large sums of money and wearing expensive jewelry. I've witnessed black kids selling drugs out of their parents' homes. How could that parent not know? The truth is that some black parents don't care. They advocate such behavior. I realize that all of this sounds unbelievable, but it's a fact. These types of black parents will not only allow their children to sell drugs out of their homes, but even try to justify their actions. Black families suffer simply because we allow our children to become the parent. At the same time we seem not to care about what our children are doing with their young lives.

Nobody said that it was easy to rear a child, and no one ever told you that you had to be a perfect parent. Sometimes a parent can do almost everything right and still have a troubled child. We would like to believe that our well-reared child simply went wrong by associating with the wrong group of their peers. Then we would like to believe that our child's bad behavior resulted from the failures of other parents. My mother used to tell me not to run with the wrong group when, in fact, I was the wrong group all by myself. Some black parents have the habit of not recognizing the problems of their own children but can clearly see what other children are doing wrong. Some of us are experts when it comes to telling other parents about how to rear their children when we have no control over our own children.

Truth: Many black teens are out of line because many black parents are out of line. Black fathers are not taking responsibility for what their sons are doing at a young age. Most teenage pregnancies take place in the home of one of the parents because we don't teach our children to know better. We tend to write it off as something that just happened. We have a need to understand that the parent's teens should be held responsible. If you have one out of four children who become a problem, then you can say that the child placed the problem upon himself. However, if you have three out of four who become problem children, then you can be very sure that the problem lies with the parents without a doubt. Most black parents don't really know their children as well as they would like to believe. We like to think that we have good children and that we are good parents. The apple doesn't fall far from the tree, and it takes good parents to correct their children's problems before things get totally out of control.

It takes good parents to understand that they are not perfect. Therefore, their children won't be perfect either. However, if we can get to know each of our children and set good examples for them, then we will at least have a chance at rearing productive children. We don't want to settle for just good children, but we want to have productive, respectable, and responsible children. Good children are the ones who are doing the killings in our schools. Good children are using and selling drugs on our streets. Good children turn bad every single day. Black America does not need any more good children, but more productive children to carry the torch toward progression. Productive children will become aggressive in getting what they have earned but will remain humble toward others.

In the book *Wisdom from the Bible,* Don and Nancy Dick wrote, "Boys will be boys." said the mother of two mischievous young children. Her boys were into everything, causing calamity wherever they went. The children would terrorize other boys and girls, but the excuse was always the same. If the pair caused injury or pain, they were rarely scolded. Their mother merely laughed it off and chalked it up to youthful exuberance.

There is a difference between the energy of youth and destructive, disruptive behavior. The curiosity of young children is wonderful; but if unwatched, it can turn to disaster. A child with a package of matches can wreak havoc. There is nothing to be gained by letting children rule their own lives. They need guidance to protect them from things which might hurt them or others.

Children, indeed, need guidance from their parents most of all. Here's another truth that must be exposed, and you won't believe this one either: Many black children are taught all the wrong things before they reach 5 years of age. They are allowed to dance in a way that is unbecoming of a child. Some black children are taught to swear or, as we say "cuss", before the innocent age of 2 years old. I have personally witnessed such behavior more times than I care to recall, and I can tell you that it is a sin before God to mislead His children. I can't begin to understand why

God would even bother to allow some people to have children in the first place! I mean that there are parents who don't deserve children. I, too, have made a ton of mistakes as a parent; but by the grace of God, I have come to truly understand the importance of my role of being a good father and husband.

I still make mistakes. However, it has been a learning experience for me. Now I can be a better grandfather. Good things come to those of us who do good things. We've got to teach what is good to our children in order to be a successful parent. All good things come from God, and it is impossible to rear productive children without the instructions from God. We are nothing without God. So, there is no way we can be successful as parents without His blessing. How can we even claim victory without God's consent and blessing? Black parents need help from somewhere because some of us are not getting the job done on our own merits. Truth: Our children deserve more than some of us are willing to offer at this point in time. Some parents are failures at being productive parents, and it shows by the way our children live.

The black parents who are baby boomers were reared up in the proper manner, and we did not do the things in which we allow our children to do today. We had no choice but to go to school and church. We had to show respect toward our elders, teachers, and everyone else. Children back then had to be a child at all times with no exceptions. Our parents were always in control, and they insisted upon maintaining order among their children. Some black parents today are not in control, and our children will suffer for that lack of control.

Most black parents today are not half the parents that their mothers and fathers were. Children today may be a bit smarter than we were as children, but they still cannot rear themselves. We support our children while they destroy everything that we've worked all of our lives to gain. Truth: The real problem with most of our black youth is our inability as parents to be parents. We just can't treat our children as equals because a child needs to remain in a child's place.

We have got to establish ourselves as the parent from the very beginning without any exceptions.

Everyday black children are being sent to prison, and we are burying our children in cemeteries all over this nation. Every day our black youth are turning against their parents only because black parents are losing the battle in rearing their children. Just when is all this madness going to end? I for one cannot answer that question for you, but I know that we would be better off if we reared our children the way we were reared.

We owe a great deal to the black parents who labor to provide for their children, and the rest of us should be doing the same for ours. Those of us who don't take out the time to rear our children properly only make it hard for the parents who do. My hat is off to the many black parents who have done the right things in rearing their children, and I pray that many more of us will realize that our children are our greatest assets.

CHAPTER 9

BLACK ON BLACK CRIME

I would have you learn this great fact, that a life of doing right is the wisest life there is. (Proverbs 4:11).

Black crime against black people does not consist of only theft, drugs, murder, and robbery. It also consists of how we treat one another. Black-on-black crime stems from jealousy, hate, and even prejudice. I am willing to stake my life on the fact that 60 percent of black people won't work for an all black company. I know this to be true, and I have got to come clean on this one. It's not only because the pay with small, black companies is substandard and below the poverty line, it's because it is near impossible for black coworkers to get along. This is one of the most common forms of black on black crime.

On the job blacks will almost every time form little groups and try to cross out one another with deceit. Many blacks in the workplace are jealous of each other and would much rather see a white person get promoted than see another black person get promoted to supervisor. Many blacks will do anything to make a black coworker look bad. Most of us do not like to take orders from a black supervisor. I cannot understand why many of us are this way. Truth: We cannot deal with racism if we cannot honestly deal with each other. First of all, we must admit to ourselves that dishonesty to other blacks is very much a black on black crime. Dishonesty is a crime that most of us display toward fellow blacks, and it has no place in our race.

White people are confused by the way we address each other and of how we turn on one another. For example, we call each other the "N" word, but we tend to get very upset when a white person says the same word. We believe that it's a difference in the use of the "N" word when it is said outside of the black race. Common sense should tell you that the "N" word has the very same meaning no matter who is using it! Many of us do not respect ourselves, but we demand respect from others. Come on now. Let's be real about how much sense any of this makes.

Here is another form of black on black crime, and it doesn't get any better as I continue on. Many black women who have gone to the Department of Human Services to receive aid of some kind in order to take care of their children can tell you some horror stories. Most of these women who go think that a black case worker would gladly be willing to help another black. Well, I can tell you of how wrong you are, and that's a well-proven fact. I know that the majority of black workers are the ones who believe that he or she is better than the person who they are paid to serve with dignity. These caseworkers are the ones who give other blacks a hard time getting help. In most cases, these women who are applying for help are entitled to receive aid for their children.

These particular caseworkers will talk down to another black as if he or she is better than the person applying for help. These caseworkers seem to think that the taxpayers' money belongs to them. In reality, it is the taxpayers' money that pays the caseworkers' salaries in the first place. Too many black people are envious who cannot stand to see another member of their race own anything in which they themselves don't own. Truth: Not all black Americans have this mentality, but most of us do. Now envy is the worst form of black on black crime. Envy is destroying our race. Why is it like that between black people? I'll tell you. It started in slavery when the white slave owners pitted the house workers against the field workers. This is when the divide and conquer started with our people. I know that it must cease before we self-destruct.

This chapter sickens me simply because there isn't any reason whatsoever why blacks kill each other on the street. This type of black on black crime is totally out of hand among our black youth. We stand idly by as if we don't notice the crime that is happening all around us daily. It doesn't have to be this way for black America. We can now live just about anywhere we choose to live, and we have a right to vote for anyone we choose. We can sit at the front of the bus today, thanks to Rosa Parks. We are legally and politically a free people, but many of us are bound by our mentality because we do envision ourselves as the American success story that history has proven.

Why must we still have the mentality of former slaves and not understand that we are a free people today and tomorrow? We are protected by the laws of our federal government. According to those laws, we are free to pursue happiness. More of us have a need to become educated and allow our children to become educated. There has got to be a decrease in black on black crime. Let us take advantage of these laws that many of our ancestors died for. There isn't any Godly reason for black America to be afraid to stand up for doing what's right within the laws of this nation. If we don't learn to stand up for something, we will always fall for anything! We cannot afford to pretend as if everything is acceptable the way it currently is.

God will not help us to progress until we decide that we want progression. Black America must want a better life for black America because there isn't anyone else who really cares. Black on black crime makes it hard for many of us to build a better future for ourselves. Many of us are confused and do not try to understand why we are behind everyone else economically and educationally. We do not deal with certain issues effectively, but at some point we have got to show that we do care.

Black on black crime is all around us. We could do a better job by making it safer where we live by not allowing crime to become the norm. We must work together toward a positive solution. There is not an excuse for not being productive, and there is no excuse for failing to control our children. It is not a good image when our youth break the law. It is a setback for our race when our youth drop out of school or sell drugs on the corner. Truth: I am saddened and feel very sorry for the hard working class of blacks who suffer the most. However, it has to be that same working people who will play a major role in pulling up others simply by demonstrating values and being an example to the rest of us.

It is not hard for me to understand the fear that the black youth place upon most of white America. It is not hard to understand why white American's afraid for blacks to move in the house next door. There are many black people who are worthy of living anywhere, but many blacks are misrepresented by those blacks who don't want anything out of life.

There are members of our race who don't want to work for their share of success in this country. My heart goes out to the black Americans who work hard at teaching their children right from wrong. Not all black parents let their children roam free.

Black America is a perfect example of the good suffering for the bad with black-on- black crime. At times white America cannot recognize a working black from a nonproductive black by just looking at him/her. The whites sometimes misjudge blacks and are afraid of them. It is unfair for black Americans to be judged by the color of their skin. There are a large number of blacks who work very hard for the right to live wherever they choose. These blacks should have that right by every means.

No race has the right to disregard the rights of others. I am not by any means implying that whites have the right to disallow blacks to live next door. However, everyone has the right to know the character of their next-door neighbor as well as the right to protect the area in which their children live and play. Everyone has the right to protect the neighborhood in which their children liven and play. Too many blacks fail to live by those rights because they allow drugs and crime to remain steadfast where their children live and play.

It may start to appear that I am ashamed to be a black American, but truly I am very proud to be a black American. I am not proud, however, of the black man I once was. I have come to understand that if I would have kept doing what I was doing, then I would have still had what I had back then, which was nothing. I had to first make a decision to change my black way of thinking, and that alone changed my black way of living. Why do I have to be considered a black truck driver, a black teacher, or a black brick layer? I prefer to be considered a truck driver, a teacher, or a brick layer. There is no reason why I have to b e distinguished by my color.

I guess when I see black youth selling drugs, dying on the street, and going to prison, I see myself in those children. I realize just where the road that they are taking will lead to. It concerns me very much because I did some of those very things. I know God really loves me a lot for me to have lived through all the dumb things I did at a young age and even at not so young of an age. A good friend of mine named Daisy Cole once told me that I had missed my calling because of how I had ruined my chances to succeed. However, I believe that writing the truth is my calling. My hope is that the rest of our black youth will realize that life is too precious and short to throw it away for a few good times. I am hard on black America simply because I am even harder on myself.

I must present you with another truth: We hold the future of black American in our own hands. Even though we are our own worst enemy and we do not cause most of our own problems, black people should not ever want to do anything that would cause them to go to jail. It is a known fact that blacks get more time in prison than whites. I am telling you that if a white person and a black person commit the very same crime on the very same day and go before the very same judge; chances are that the black person will receive a stiffer sentence. Now, the truth goes both ways, by knowing that fact to be true, why would put yourself in harm's way?

This book is not by any means anti-black, and I do not want it to appear that way at all. My only purpose is for my book to be anti-ignorant for my people. I realize that the fire has gotten hot and I am about to put both hands in it (ouch). Are we no smarter than we pretend to be? Black America has to grow up and begin to smell the coffee at least for the sake of our children. I don't dislike my race, but I dislike the apathy we have for our children. I dislike the lack of love, concern, and respect we show toward each other.

Black on black crime has become a burden to black America, and it must be addressed or there won't be a bright future for us anytime soon. For some of us, every step of progress we make, we take three steps backwards; and that, regressing. Some of us are blind when it comes to seeing just what we are doing to ourselves and to our children. Some cannot seem to understand that we are the major cause of most of our problems. I know that we can overcome the white man, but can we overcome ourselves? Maybe just my bringing out the whole truth will shock some into reality. Just maybe some will realize the possibility of progression for us all. We might realize the reality of our dreams by understanding where we are right now.

I have high hopes that black America will turn to God. While turning to God, God will honor our positive desires of black Americans. There are just too many blacks who are successful for me not to know that I can do the same. I cannot be happy with only myself doing better, but also for other black Americans who want the same things. As for those of us who are just happy to be alive, then there is nothing in I can say or do that will make a difference in their lives. Some of black America hasn't suffered enough. Blacks who are not helping those blacks that need help are committing a black on black crime. It is not only a crime to break the law, but it is immoral not to help your fellow man who deserves your help.

Some want to believe that suffering allows them to be closer to God. Some believe that suffering brings about blessings. These people believe that the longer they suffer, the bigger the blessing. God does not want to see us suffer in life. However, if we suffer for His name sake, then we will be blessed. I do not know what God you are worshipping, but my God is a loving, understanding, and forgiving God. I know that every day is not bright, and I realize that there will be pain in everyone's life at one time or another. It is not because God wants it that way. It is because we want to suffer by not doing what is right. My God does not want to see black America hurt, but many of us refuse to take heed to His word. God will not bless our race until we humble ourselves before Him and forgive the white race for slavery. We have to forgive in order to be forgiven and blesses.

Truth: We have got to forgive the white race with all of our heart, soul, and mind for everything that they have done to the black race through the years. We need to forgive those of the white race who offend us in the future. The black race is very much oppressed today, but we are still here. So, why can't our presence be known? Just like the freedom riders once said, "If not us, then who?" "If not now, when?" We haven't any more time to waste. We must put an end to black on black crime before it's too late. Hurt, pain, hate, and backbiting are no way of God. He calls upon all races to love and respect each other. He wants all people to live on this earth in peace and harmony.

If we cannot show some kind of love to our own people and others, then we bear a false witness to Jesus. Black on black crime will always place darkness upon any efforts of black America to progress toward becoming a respectful people. (Proverbs 4:18) "But the path of the just is as the shining light, that shine more and more unto the perfect day." The only way we are to see that perfect day of progression is to be a just people and allow God to help us. Allow God to help each of us to understand our part in His perfect plan for us. If God did not have a plan for blacks in America, we would not be her in the first place. Now that we are here, let us become a productive part of this great nation.

CHAPTER 10

OUR BLACK GOVERNMENT

How long wilt thou sleep, O sluggard? When wilt thou arise out of thy sleep?

(Proverbs 6:9)

Is it that black America has missed out on so much because we refuse to awaken to the reality of our misdeeds? It is our own undoing in which has led to our failures in America. Just how long will our people remain sleep, O sluggard? Are we unable to awaken from the sleep of disparity, O sluggard? We can't bring ourselves to understand the seriousness of not dealing with our setbacks. Since black America insist upon doing things our own way, then it is safe for me to say that we are governed by our own government. Thus, we have our own form of government for black people and by black people. We live by the rules of our black government while the rest of America is moving ahead to a better way of life.

Truth: We are governed by the NAACP, black Baptist, and everything else that is black. We have the black pages instead of the yellow pages. We learn black, breath black, eat black, and we live black as well. Now it's to my understanding that Dr. Martin Luther King, Jr. gave his life for blacks to be considered equal. But today some of us separate ourselves from the white race and surround ourselves with everything that is black. We fight for the little things that won't make a difference one way or another toward the progression for us in America.

Our black way of life is not serving any purpose for us because it simply does not work for the good of our people. I believe that progress will come a lot quicker only if we play by the same rules as the rest of America and get on the same page. We cannot make our own rules and keep up with white America at the same time. Dr. King had a dream that black America would be allowed to achieve as much as white America on equal terms. He had a dream that black people would reach the promise land of equality. Dr. King's dream is very much possible, but only if we work together toward solutions to the problems within our race.

I have love, respect, and admiration for Dr. King, and I can only hope to become just a small part of the man he was. Dr. King was not a man seeking recognition, but a man whom wanted a better America for his family and his people. I truly respect a man who will give up his life and leave behind a beautiful wife and children for me. Dr. King wasn't trying to form a black government. He wanted to reform the existing government and the laws of that government in order to include black people. Dr. King was chosen by God to die for what he believed to be right for us. If it were at all possible for Dr. King to come back to us, he would come back and risk his life all over again for people who won't help themselves!

Dr. King would want black America to realize his dream and make it our own dream. He did not intend for us to have a government within our race. Dr. King wanted us to become an equal part of the American government that was always in place. We have got to become a part of the American system before there to be a change within the system. There is a need for black Americans to vote in bigger numbers. More blacks have to run for public office. It is much easier to have a voice when you are on the inside that it is to be heard from the outside.

Now it's time again to be truthful, and I know that I'll get a lot of backlash from this one. (oh, well) I know for a fact there's at least a few blacks who may agree with me on this. 'There is no way possible at this stage of my life that I would remotely ponder the idea of living in an all black state even here in the United States. Let's just say that this all black state was governed by all black people. Well, the answer is double no. I won't consider living there! The reason being is mostly because of the crime rate and because we are not idealistic, and we can't survive each other. We can't at this time govern ourselves without enlisting the help of white America. Blacks in America have become dependent upon whites, and it is a proven fact that we cannot function without their input or aid.

Some of us live like a lost people in the ghettos. We rob, rape, and kill each other as if we are above the laws of this nation. We then wonder why our nation's prisons are so overcrowded with young, black men. We can't seem to begin to understand why white America tries to move away from us. There are black Americans who are escaping the crime and confusion of the inner city. There are also a great many blacks who are afraid for their children in all-black areas throughout America.

Now, back to the all black state that is to be governed by all black people. Just try for a moment to imagine (close your eyes) that we are given an all black state about the size of Texas or larger. This large area will be occupied by all black people, and there will be no outside help from anyone. Are you still with me on this? Now consider living there with your children and consider rearing them there. I am only being truthful about the way I feel about all of this, and I know that many other blacks share the very same feelings as I do.

I am no longer in denial about who we really are in America and where we stand as a people in America. I fully accept the truth about what it really means to be a black man in America. White people haven't any realistic idea, not even a clue as to what a black man has to endure in this country. We should not be totally blamed for our economic positions. However, we are part to blame, and we must own up to our part. Sure blacks are not always treated equally, and we are often passed up for job promotions. Black people are often overlooked, mistreated, and are unfairly judged because of our dark skin color; but those should be the reasons for black America to want to move up the economic ladder and overcome the stereotypes placed upon us and our children. It is up to us if we are to overcome all which is against us. I mean that it's not like any of this is new to any of us. So, what's the problem with dealing with racism?

Why should we allow the ignorance of hateful people to prevent us from becoming a productive part of mainstream America? Yes, we have a need to govern ourselves as black people, but we are to be governed within the system that is already in place and according to the laws of our nation. The only black governing we need is to bring about control of our children and our race.

God created all men equal, and nobody can convince me of anything else. No man has the right to stop another man from being productive in the United States of America. We are one people in the eyes of God, and that standard was set by God. The beginning and the ending of all things is God. So, why allow anyone to disallow you whatever there is for you? Blacks have been governed by white America since slavery, but the laws have long since changed. It is now time for us to change. Black America is no longer limited like the slaves. We may have to work harder than whites in order to achieve the same goals. After all, we have not started from a level field with the whites. However, we must be willing to do whatever it takes for however long it takes to become successful.

God is who will judge us after death, and you have Him to thank for that. Death is the only sure thing in which we will face, and everything else is only by chance. Without a doubt, blacks are different from whites. However, we are not, by any means, less than anyone on God's green earth. What we really need is to be governed by God and be rooted in His word so that we can reap His blessings. We have no true leadership in the black race to get things done. I mean that the blind can't lead the blind. They both would fall in the ditch. If a person with no brain would share the love he has in his heart with a person with no heart, then both of them would have a better chance of becoming successful. The moral of this story is that no matter what our plights in life are, we can somehow work together as one. We can still get the job done.

I hope that now maybe you can understand what I am trying to tell you. It's going to take all kinds of black people to help us conquer our fears. We must learn to help those members of black America who are poor and in need of help. We must look out for those who are not educated and show love to those members who need friends. Black America should govern ourselves for the right reasons and not step on anyone along the way. Truth: It is the responsibility of black America to make things better for black America! No one owes us anything except a fair chance. If for any reason you are not afforded a fair chance, then take whatever chance there is to become successful.

The math in all of this is very simple, and it's easy as one plus one. One idea plus one solution equals one better black America and one prosperous black America, which is two. Now you see that two heads are always better than one any day. Just think about a thousand black people putting all their heads together for one purpose. Truth: That is what whites were afraid of during slavery, and that holds true in many instances today. The less we know, the less we are feared! If we can become as one race of productive people, the walls of repression will have to come down. There is no other way for black America to become a productive force in this country. I can tell you today that we are at the door of prosperity in America, and all that is left is to kick the sucker down with unity.

A successful black America must consist of every willing and productive black person. There is the need for those blacks who are educated to build up the esteem of those blacks who are lacking a proper education. The strong and wise blacks must lift up those blacks who are weak and close-minded. This is the message that we should be hearing from Jesse Jackson and Al Sharpton, but they tell black America just what it wants to hear. The reality of it is that right now black America really stinks. I will tell you just what blacks need to hear and not what they want to hear because I'm not running for any office. This is what I don't like about our self-appointed black leaders. They mislead their own people by placing blame on others and by not telling us that we should hold ourselves accountable for our problems.

One hand washes the other in the sense that we are all in the same boat of oppression and have the need to help each other. It does not matter what social status we come from. We are all considered the same in the eyes of most white Americans. It is about being honest with ourselves and doing what is right for all black people. "Even a child is known by his doings, whether his work be pure, and whether it be right." (Proverbs 20:11) We all know right from wrong. It's just a matter of doing what is right.

The truth is that blacks were brought to this country against their will, and they were worked from sunup to sundown. They were fed discarded food from white slave-owners, treated less than livestock in which they tended. Their children were sold like animals at the market, and black women were beaten and raped at will by white owners and his buddies. Slaves were chained like common criminals and hung from trees on a daily basis. Are you getting a little angry at the white man? Then stop making excuses, and let's make some progress. If you are a little upset at the way slaves were treated, then let's take our rightful in America. Let's progress the right way by doing what is right.

Black slaves were not treated fairly by any means, and most slave-owners were evil in those days. They were a people from hell and hated black people for just being black. However the odds, black uneducated slaves pulled together and sought freedom through spiritual songs that they sang together while working in the fields. Even the slaves had a government in the form of survival. They could have easily given up on becoming free, but they continued to run away from plantations all over America. We are free today, but some appear to have given up and don't seem to care one bit about our future. Blacks today are not faced with dealing with slavery, and there is nothing in the way to stop us from becoming a productive and great people. Those who were slaves before we were born have paved the way through their blood, sweat, and tears.

Black America today is enslaved by the decisions that we make every day. Slavery today comes from black on black crime, drug addiction, and a lack of education! I bet that Jesse Jackson will not tell black America that we are self-produced slaves because of low self-esteem and lack of pride within our race. Some blacks today are self-applied slaves because some of us refuse to govern ourselves and our children. Is there an end to our self-created mayhem? Only we can possibly answer that question, but are we willing to answer that question any time soon? Another question is: Will we continue to administer limitations on ourselves without any abandonment?

The reason that so many blacks are so far behind civilization is because we are not the whole truth, and we don't represent the truth even to each other. We can't be true to ourselves, and we continue to live a lie. That lie is that it's always someone else's fault. We are led to believe the lie that the white man is totally responsible for our being held back. There are a great deal of blacks who remain among the poorest of Americans while some of us are experiencing success. Why is there so many of us living as poor folks in such a rich country? A small part of the reason is that many black folk are oppressed by racism, and I will admit that. However, we are our own worst enemy; and until we face up to that truth, we will continue to regress even more.

I will not give in to oppression, racism, or to my own undoing because my family depends on me to provide for them. Jesus holds the truth for all people, and black America has to seek that truth. Truth: No one can hurt black America but black America, and no one can help black America but black America. It all depends on how we govern ourselves and our leadership. A productive black leader can only help us in our endeavor to become successful and move forward. There must be one form of government, meaning that all of our black organizations should become as one well-oiled machine. What we don't need is a bunch of nonproductive black organizations causing havoc among our people. One united, black organization would better serve blacks and aid us in becoming a productive part of our existing government.

David G. Bowman

We don't need just any form of a black government, but a black aggressive government that is a part of the American government. We must be a united organization that will demand to be heard and demand that changes be made in the existing American government, changes that will support the idea of a free and equal America. Black America has a need for leadership that represents truth, honor, and foremost, the black American people. We need leadership in which will be respected by all people throughout the whole world. There cannot be but one government in this country. However, it has to be a government that will support all people no matter their race, color, or creed. The government of the United States needs to be adjusted to include black Americans. We are not true Americans until we can partake of the American dream. I will leave you with this: We cannot justify being in Iraq until we treat everyone the same in this country. Black Americans must find solutions for ourselves and not depend upon our government to make it right for us. Think about it.

CHAPTER 11

BLACKS IN SPORTS

"Then shall thou understand righteousness, and judgment, and equity; yea, every good path. (Proverbs 2:8)

Black professional athletes are looked up to by black youth more than any other black professionals. They have a responsibility to uphold good standards for their fans, but the parents are even more responsible than anyone else to set good examples for their young children.

It is only fitting that I begin this chapter with O.J. Simpson's trial. It would not be fair for me to pass any kind of judgment upon Mr. Simpson, but I can say what I know to be the truth. Black America rallied around O.J., and it didn't matter one bit to us if he killed those two people or not. Now whenever a black person is beaten by the police or killed by a white person, we tend to get very upset, to say the least. We come out in great numbers, looking for any white person available to hurt or something to destroy. However, when it's one of us who is doing the killing, we tend to accept it as a part of life. I am not suggesting that O.J. had anything to do with killing those people because I don't want to believe that he could do such a horrible crime.

We did not learn a single lesson from the O.J. case, and we did not even consider right or wrong at any given time. All we saw was that a black hero was being accused by the white man, and we thought him to be abused by a mostly white system. I can't seem to understand our personal attachment to the O.J. Simpson verdict. Of all the murders in this country, 49 percent are blacks; and of that 49 percent of blacks who are murdered a staggering 90 percent is killed by other blacks.

Blacks, we have a need to do something about black on black crime. Where is the NAACP when blacks are killing blacks? Why aren't they in front of the cameras pleading with black youth to stop killing each other? Does the NAACP only value black lives when one of us are killed by a white person?

Truth: There are over 20 times more blacks killed by one another than there are killed by whites. We easily accept the fact that we rape, murder, rob, and assault our own people. However, black America gets offended when a white person does the very same things to one of us. I don't understand our reaction to the O.J. Simpson verdict. Black America seems not to care anything about the people who was murdered because a black was accused of killing two whites. We could only see that a black man was on trial for something he didn't do. Now, I am not a genius, but I know that black America wasn't looking at both sides of the coin. It's like my brother can kill somebody, but you can't kill my brother. However, it's all right for my brother to murder; but it's wrong for you to murder. Does any of that make sense? Of course if doesn't make any sense whatsoever, but that's what we believe.

I'm a little confused myself. Like I said, blacks didn't learn or gain a single thing from the O.J. Simpson case. Neither did we accomplish anything from the verdict. The entire black race lost because of the way we carried ourselves in from of the whole world. O.J. was my hero, as well, and it hurt me to see him in jail; but I could only pray that justice would eventually prevail for him. Blacks demand justice, and we should want what is already automatic for all other Americans. We must also want justice for others and treat other people equally as well. If we want to be heard, then we must also listen to others before forming an opinion of our own. We will not get anything in return if our demands are not just.

Let's move on to Michael Jordan because I am getting depressed from writing about the O.J. Simpson trial. I really want to be like Mike but not only because of money and fame, even though those are factors. I want to simply be like Mike because of the way he represents himself in the public. Mike is truly a role model and is very much loved by black and white kids alike. Mike used his basketball skills to close the gap of racism in America. Black America needs more Mikes and black men like him to be role models. Mike is one of a kind, and there will never be another like him. That is true for everyone because we are all one of a kind and there is no one just like you.

I believe that each of us processes some type of skill in order to help close the gap of racism in this country. We may never become a basketball icon, but we can do our part with whatever skills we do have to help this country get better. We all should want to be like Mike and give our children someone to look up to as role models.

My number one role model is my maternal grandfather Humphrey Warner, Sr., better known as Papa. He had very little formal education, but his wisdom was impeccable. For instance, he would always tell me to save my money. He would say, "Money is like chicken teeth." Papa was a master carpenter who built most of his children's houses on the land that he owned free and clear. He set his children in an economic position from the start, for the ones he built homes for did not have to worry about mortgages. The examples that Papa set for his children and grandchildren are priceless. I really didn't feel the impact of his way of life until I was a grown man. Not only was he great to me, but he was one of the most respected men in DeQuincy, Louisiana. I am quite sure that there are many other role models in our communities. We have to just pay attention. It makes a difference when you can sit and talk to someone rather than just hear about them on the news or see them on television.

Let's move on to Mike Tyson. Mike Tyson seems, who many believe, to be a lost cause; but I refuse to believe that Tyson does not have any good in him. After all, he did give all of his money away. Mike Tyson is a prime example of being your own worst enemy. However, he didn't cause all of his downfalls by himself. Here comes a big truth, and I have to tell that truth, even it it's in favor of Mike Tyson. Boxing is a brutal sport, and the heavyweight class is dominated by blacks. There are still chants of Rocky by white America. There is a great deal of racism within the sport of boxing, as we all very well know.

Mike Tyson is and has been a target not only by whites, but also by some blacks. Mike does not use good judgment and is in need of representation by a well-respected person, such as Magic Johnson who befriended him at one time. Yes, there are people who are out to derail Tyson, but Mike always finds a way to make their job easy. Mike Tyson is not a role model. As a matter of fact, he shows black youth what not to do. Black America is praying, and most are pulling for Mike to make a change in his life. But he has to accept Jesus Christ as the Son of God, and there isn't any need to say more.

Magic Johnson has always been a good role model for our children. He set aside the negative reaction of America in order to shed a realistic light on the HIV virus among blacks. I, for one, truly respect him for setting aside his personal feelings and the feelings of his family in order to make blacks understand that AIDS can happen to anyone. We all love Magic Johnson, and we thank God for all he has done for his race. Magic was at the side of Mike Tyson during Mike's reinstatement hearing so that Mike could continue to be a fighter. Mr. Johnson has not forgotten where he came from like many other famous blacks have done.

Dennis Rodman, Dennis Rodman, Dennis Rodman. This man must have been dropped from a four-story building on his head as an infant. There is no other explanation for his being so different from the rest of the human race. I can't help but love the guy, but there is no earthly reason for Dennis being like he is. He is a professional basketball player, for God's sake, but he insist upon being a clown at the same time. I hope that one day soon Dennis will return to the NBA and do what he does best.

Deion Sanders, formally with the Dallas Cowboys, has become one of my favorites because he has learned to love the rest of the world as much as we all love him. It's not like he did all of this love on his own. Deion accepted Jesus Christ as his Lord and Savior, and now I enjoy watching him on game day. I will never attempt to put Deion Sanders down because he came to realize that this thing is bigger than himself, and he made a change in his life by giving it to God. That was the longest runback he ever made for a touchdown when he ran into the end zone of Jesus.

There was a time when I was full of it also; and I, too, decided to let go and let God like Deion Sanders did. It's not about me, and it's not about any one person, as far as that goes. We are all living on borrowed time, and we should try to make the best of what we have. I mean that our own life does not belong to us, so why waste time worrying about others? Our homes, cars, money, and even our children are a loan from God. Mr. Sanders now understands that he was nothing without God in his life. We are all naked before God, and He can see through each and every one of us! I would hate to be a racist when I go before God for judgment, and that is all we have to know. Anything that we have is a gift from God because He loves us so much.

Black America must stop deeming ourselves the only victims in America and start doing for ourselves. It is our choice that determines our future as a race. Black youth need black role models to show them that being black hasn't got anything to do with failure. We are not bound to failure by the color of our skin nor held back because of racism alone. We truly have our future in our own hands, and nobody can stop us if we apply ourselves. We can go from victims to victors by believing in each other and working toward progression.

Reggie White formerly of the Green Bay Packers is also a role model for our young people, and he sets good examples. Rev. White lives his life by the word of God, and he is a blessing to black America. Reggie has an all-pro football career in the NFL and he gives all the glory to Jesus. Rev. White had his church burned down to the ground, and he did not go public, blaming white folks. He gave it to God, and he did not take matters into his own hands as we did with Rodney King and the OJ Simpson trial. Rev. White did not want any fanfare nor any undue publicity.

Henry "Hank" Aaron brought America to their feet when he broke Babe Ruth's homerun record. Black youth had a new hero to look up to at that time, and I still look up to him. Atlanta, Georgia is a mostly black city. However, the new stadium was not named after Hank Aaron, but Turner "The Ted" Field instead. The street that runs in front of Turner Field was named to honor Hank Aaron. However, there was a high school field in Mobile, Alabama named to honor Hank; and he was there for the great honor. Henry Hank Aaron is a classy classical guy, and he deserves everything he has received for all he has done for all America. Thank you, Hank.

There is no limit to what blacks can accomplish when we really put our minds to what we want to do. We are a blessed people, but we must accept our blessing by doing what is right unto God. We must first help ourselves and stop whining about what we don't have versus what whites do have. I personally am not going to be outdone, and I won't give in under any circumstances. If we can become good to ourselves, then we will become good to others. When we become good to others, then God will become good to black America. When God becomes good to us, only then will we live a prosperous life, and only then will God call us His people.

Tiger Woods may become the greatest golfer ever to play the game, and he has already climbed to the top of what used to be an all-white sport. The only reason golf was considered a white man sport is because blacks and women were not allowed on the course at one time in history. Tiger Woods won the Masters and was fitted with a green jacket. Most of black America tuned in on the final of that Masters to cheer Tiger to victory. Some of us had never watched a single round of golf before in our lives. Tiger is an inspiration to the black youth because of his accomplishments.

Cynthia Cooper of the Houston Comets is called "The Michael Jordan" of Women's Professional Basketball. In her first three years of play, she -- along with her teammates -- won three championships. Now young black girls have hopes of becoming a professional basketball player in the WNBA. Sheryl Swoops and Monica Lamb are also members of the Comets. All three ladies are role models, and they give our children someone to look up to.

George Foreman is the oldest heavyweight champion in the history of boxing. Rev. Foreman represents what a black man should be in America, and he will be the first to tell you just how proud he is to be an American. There is no doubt that Big George is very proud of being a black American. When it comes to dealing with racism, Rev. Foreman will let the Lord fight his battles; and that is the reason he became a champion at an older age.

Daryl Strawberry played baseball for the New York Mets and the New York Yankees. He has three championship rings to his credit, but Daryl is not as good to himself as he was to baseball. He is a drug addict, and will be until he can own up to his actions. He had everything going his way until he made the decision to use drugs. Because of drugs, he lost almost everything. The world owes you nothing, and the world will only give you back whatever you have coming. Daryl Strawberry was a great baseball player, and I hope that he can simply regain the life that was meant for him.

Black parents must set examples for their children and do our best in rearing our children to be independent. Young children must learn from their parents as we did from our parents. Black sport professionals are not responsible for rearing our children. It is up to the parents to teach their own children to want to be successful.

CHAPTER 12

LET GO AND LET GOD

If anyone does not love the Lord, that person is cursed. (I Corinthians 16:22)

There was a time when blacks worshipped God with all of their heart, soul, and mind. During the days of slavery, we were at the mercy of slave-owners; but we still worshipped God day and night. How long can black America hold on to the horrors of slavery, and how long can we harbor our past? I believe that the past is the past and should be used to teach our children about the struggle it took to get us where we are today. If the past is not left behind, then we will certainly remain slaves to it. Now is the time to let go and let God be our redeemer.

"The simple believes every word, but the prudent man looks well to his going." (Proverbs 14:15) It is in the best interest of black America to look where we are going and not be overly concerned about what is left behind us. Simple people dwell upon their past, but prudent people look to what may be ahead. Black America must not worry about the small things in which we may confront from day to day. We must prepare ourselves for what tomorrow may bring. We have got to depend upon the word of God to uplift us in times of trouble and allow God to fight even our small battles for us daily. This is what the black churches should be teaching, and that is what we need to practice.

God has not forsaken black America. It's that black America has forsaken God. We have taken the fight from God and made a plum mess of things. Rev. Dr. Martin Luther King was chosen by God to do the will of God. Dr. King gladly complied with God's will until his death. The will of a man won't begin to progress blacks, so why should we follow the will of man? We worry about the white race entirely too much instead of making ourselves a better people. God wants us to love even the racists and not allow hate to enter into our hearts. Love is part of God's commandments, and that's why God has the black clergy, preaching about love.

The real tragedy of all of this is that it's some of our black clergymen who lead our people into worthless marches, demanding unreasonable rights, such as the removal of the confederate flag in South Carolina. These clergymen should be preaching love, acceptance, and peace. Instead we are concerned about a flag that has been around for over 100 years, and not until now we are offended by it. Now tell me just what will black's gain by the removal of the confederate flag? Or better still, what would we have lost by not ever being concerned about the flag in the first place? If we were to display some concern toward a better black society, then we can start by realizing that the economic gap between black America and white America has not narrowed since the civil rights movement. We can start to visualize an economically stronger black America.

We have a great need to let go of slavery and allow God to start our healing process toward becoming a better race of people in America. Truth: There is no bandage big enough to stop the bleeding from the self-inflicted wounds of black America. There is no simple, short term solution to the problems within black America. The wounds are far too many to apply a bandage and believe that to be enough.

I have a 40-year plan in which will show great strides toward progression. By the time a child is 2 years of age, his or her attitude is already formed. What we teach that child over the next three years will, more or less, remain with that child for life. We will not gain anything if we don't start rearing that child according to the word of God. We must start to focus more upon children born between the years 2000 and beyond because these children will make up about 60 percent of our total population and 80 percent of any progress made by black Americans. We must instill absolute standards for behavior, and there will be no excuses for any transgressions. If there is any chance to reach those children and teach them to respect others, then black America will reap progress in 40 years. The reason being is that those same children will be the generations assuming control of our government.

There isn't any short-term plan which can be put in place in order to alter the damage within black America. It took years of regression, oppression, and discrimination against blacks for us to fall behind; and I promise you that it will take as many or more years for blacks to overcome poverty. First, we must overcome ourselves and each other in order to achieve our goals. We can achieve our goals by allowing God to be a part of our plans. We cannot blame another race for our problems because the negative numbers are against us. Those negative numbers consist of black on black crime and the number of young blacks in prison. We cannot overcome when so many members of the black society are not being accountable.

Racism is not the whole problem. Even though it plays a role in the fact that so many blacks are struggling today. However, racism is not the problem that should stop our progress because many blacks have struggled all the way to success. We can make racism more of a problem for the racist if we would not yield in any way toward racism. Just knowing that racism is out there to stop us should be motivation enough for us to achieve our every endeavor in America. We experience some type of racism almost every day of our lives. We should not allow it to alter our goals nor our way of thinking toward achieving those goals. We must refuse to hate back. When we do this, God will forever be a part of our struggle.

It is important that black people understand that without the approval of God, our plans will fail. Without the approval of God, we are going to fail. Without the approval of God, we will not achieve success with His blessing. So, therefore any success for us will be short-lived. We must humble ourselves before the Lord and find it in our hearts to forgive even those who dislike the color of our skin. Blacks must not allow others to define us by what they may think about us. We must learn to love even those who hate us for who God made us to be. God calls upon all churches to preach love toward our enemies. God demands that all churches preach that we pray even for our oppressors. All churches have a responsibility not only to preach salvation, but also to preach love for our fellow man.

Some blacks are also guilty of racism and violate the rights of white Americans. Now, many of us want to hear the truth, but be it as it may, I have sworn to tell the truth. I will honor my promise no matter what. Black America is quick to holler, "foul" on someone else's court, but we are not accountable whenever we are the ones who are doing the fouling. We are at times just as guilty as the racist when we use our color as an excuse to have our way. When you seek racism, you'll easily find it because racism has been around since the beginning of time for man. Racism will never go away, and it will remain no matter what anyone does to prevent it.

There is but one answer to racism, and that is for it to become the end of time for mankind -- period. Blacks have to trust in God to guide us through the storms of injustice. We were not treated fairly during slavery, and we are not being treated fairly today. However, today we have many more rights to work with. We have more opportunities than ever before. Dr. King has not died in vain, but black America has to stop bringing out old, dirty laundry of our past. We've got to let go of those old days when we were slaves and look forward to the days of progression. In James 4:2 it says, "Ye have not because ye ask not." Without God, not any race of people can endure, but the seed of God shall be prosperous every time.

Look at what is said in Revelation 21:3 & 4. "And I heard a great voice out of heaven saying, behold, the tabernacle of God is with men, and He will dwell with them, and He shall with them and be their God. And God shall wipe all tears from their eyes, and there shall be no more death, neither sorrow, neither crying, neither shall there be no more pain, for former things are passed away." That is the only time in which there will be no more racism, and that is the time we all should be looking forward to see.

There isn't anything that God won't do for His people, but we must become His people! We are very much in need of God's help because we cannot rid the world of racism. Only God has the power to do so, but not until former things are passed away. There is a need to fight for equal rights for our people, but no one will ever take us seriously until we can become united as a strong people. Here in Mark 10:27 Jesus said, "With men it is impossible, but not with God, for all things are possible." Black America must let go and allow God to do our bidding for us.

It is all so very simple. We must become more active in our government. Our goal should be to have more black homeowners, better jobs, and become more educated. One of our goals should be to decrease the number of black youth dropping out of school. Another one should be to decrease the number of black men going to prison. There are many problems within our race that will not allow us the time to dwell on racism. We must fight the good fight of faith. We must let go and let God!

CHAPTER 13

FROM THE MOUTH OF A BABY

Sometimes it pays to listen to our children because I believe that they are closer to God than grownups. As parents we tend not to realize just how smart our children really are. I was reading the opinion page in the *Daily Advertiser* (April 28, 2000) which is a Lafayette, Louisiana newspaper. I was impressed by an editorial written by a 6th grader from Paul Breaux Middle School. Here's what this bright child had to say:

> "Here today in our mixed-up society, there is criticism and disagreement left and right. So much racism and hateful people out there. Why Should they make a difference? We are really All the same people despite our color, personality, thoughts, and looks. But that's the best part of us. I mean it's not always bad to be different. The differences I'm talking about are view points from other people towards others. If we all had the same personality, all looked the same, and all did the same things, then this would be one boring world. Look at all these little organizations developed by hateful people. I just don't understand why we can't all get along.

I get along with everyone -- white, black, Chinese, boy, girl, anyone. I don't make a difference at all. I look at everyone the same way that I would want to be treated. I wouldn't want to raise my children to be raised and brought up in such a confusing world, and I know that all of you parents out there wouldn't want your child to be brought up like that.

But, yet, some of you don't understand that the way you treat others and talk in front of your children could ruin their childhood and their minds. I just hope that you all understand what I am trying to get through to you. I just wish that we could all make this a better place."

Kendra Darby
6th Grade
Paul Breaux Middle School

Black children are our greatest asset toward any restoration of black America. I mean that even Stevie Wonder can see that fact, and I'm not saying that to be funny in any way. It's really a no brainer, and I believe in today's young people, regardless of color. It's that we as parents, for the most part, set poor examples for our children to follow. Our children are smart enough to know that we are not doing what's right. So, they figure why should they do what is right?

Maybe parents can learn a few things from their children and become better parents. Our children have outgrown our way of thinking, and I mean, after all, it's the year 2000. Parents today are still rearing their children like they were reared. Wake up, black parents, and get a grip. Become a part of something constructive for the sake of your children. Aid them in becoming more useful Americans. Many of us have let our children down because we have let ourselves down by not being part of our children's lives.

I pray that maybe one day that someone with the concern of the welfare of the human race, such as Kendra Darby, can become president of this great country. The reason that this country is not as great as it could become is because we do not respect each other's skin color. We do not respect each other's points of view, nor do we show the love granted to every person by God the all mighty.

As Kendra has said, "We are really all the same people, despite our color." Now that just goes to prove that a 6th grader knows more than a lot of grownups. Hopefully we grownups can begin to build upon the viewpoint of a child. I have never met Kendra, but she is a very smart, young lady. I know that there are other children out there just like her. "I just don't understand why we can't all get along." Thank you, Kendra Darby.

CHAPTER 14

BLACK AMERICANS REACTS TO 9/11

WASHINGTON-TERRORIST HIJACKS U.S. COMMERCIAL JETS (9/11/01) AND HURTLED THEM INTO THE PENTAGON AND NEW YORK'S WORLD TRADE CENTER IN A FIERY COORDINATED ATTACK THAT HAS KILLED THOUSANDS AND STUNNED A DISBELIEVING NATION, INCLUDING BLACK AMERICANS. (*Florida Times Union*)

President Bush addressed the nation in sorrow by saying, "Terrorist attacks can shake the foundations of our biggest buildings, but they cannot touch the foundation of America." Bush continued, "These acts shatter steel, but they cannot dent the steel of American resolve."

Black America was both shocked and sorrowful for the events in which took place on September 11, 2001. For the very first time, many of us came to terms with what it really means to be an American. We truly understood what a great country we all live in today and the definition of the importance of total freedom. Black Americans felt a part of this nation, some for the very first time. We became "One nation under God" overnight.

Black America began to pour into places of worship by the thousands, praying for a wounded nation and praying for their fallen countrymen and women. For the first time ever in our nation's history, black and white became grey. For a brief moment color and race did not matter. It became time for all Americans to unite and pray for our nation. Black and white Americans were equal for a very brief moment, a moment in which will be forever remembered by many black people. It took thousands of innocent lives to bring us to the realization that race is not important and that we are all Americans. However, as time began to heal our wounds, America went back to her old ways of discrimination. Black against white, white against black, and black against black. Some things in life may seem to get better but will never change.

Black America felt as helpless as the rest of America as the death toll began to rise after the 9/11 attack. We stood steadfast, watching every newscast, reading every newspaper in order to stay abreast of the aftermath of this tragic and senseless attack.

September 11, 2001 was to be a promising day for my son, Terrance. It was his 21st birthday, a day he'll never forget as long as he lives. It was a day marred by unforgiving tragic and death. Now, as his special day approaches, the reminder of that fatal attack haunts him all over again. The Olympic bombing took place in Atlanta, Georgia on July 27, 1996, the day I was to celebrate my 40th birthday. So, I can't help but wonder what might take place on December 19th, my wife's birthday or October 30th, my daughter's birthday.

During the waking hours after the destruction of the World Trade Center, racism was set aside as black and white Americans embraced one another's pain. This was a first during any of our lifetimes, and it was something good, but too good to have a long term, positive outcome for America. I would guess that 80 percent of Americans are not racist. Here's the problem: Sixty percent of that 80 percent is not concerned one way or the other about the racism which plagues America. Add that to the 20 percent of Americans who are racists (black and white), and that gives us a total of 80 percent of Americans who are responsible for America's racism. You do the math. Now that's 20 percent directly responsible and 60 percent indirectly responsible for not standing up against racism, thereby giving us a whopping 80 percent of nonproductive Americans toward ending racism in this country. This is too great a number for even a free country to overcome.

We need self-applied affirmative action in America in order to put even a dent in our country's racism. We have a need to honor the victims of 9/11 by becoming one united nation. We must become "we the people" in America, land of the free" (free to be who you are), and "home of the

77

brave (brave enough to stand up against racism). Black America has a need to establish ourselves as an asset in this country instead of an ungoverned people with too many unsolved problems within our race.

Before I continue any further, I would like to express my heartfelt condolences to the families of the victims of September 11, 2001. Your family members are heroes in every sense of the word. Black America honors those who died in the bombing of our World Trade Center and our Pentagon. May the grace of God fall upon the families of the victims, and may there be a brighter day ahead as the love of God abounds. May he give you strength and peace in order that you make it through each and every day without hate or pain in your hearts. Love one another as God loves you, for God will have the final say in all we do in the wake of our sorrows.

I will share with you the word of God (Life Recovery Bible). I Corinthians 13:4-6. "Love is patient and kind, never jealous or envious, never boastful or proud, never haughty or selfish or rude. Love does not demand its own way. It's not irritable or touchy. It does not hold grudges and will hardly even notice when others do wrong. It is never glad about injustice, but rejoices whenever truth wins out."

I realize that 9/11 hurt us deeply and that we have a need to distance ourselves from the lingering pain; but before we can move on as a nation, we must turn our lives over to the will and care of God. This country needs God to put us back on the right path. Life can be good again, but only when we put prayer back in our homes first, then our schools, and places of employment. America has a debt to pay for her wrongful past. Slavery of black Americans was very wrong. However, we must forgive those who enslaved us. None of white Americans living today was even born during slavery. Therefore, we cannot place blame on any of them. I believe that a debt is owed to black America but should be paid in the form of education, land, and tax exemptions. I am proud to be black, and I am proud of black history. Regardless of what was done to us in the past, we are still here!

The bombing of the World Trade Center and the Pentagon was equally wrong, and someone had to pay for the lives that were lost. However, we must move on from that unjustly evil. May God keep us all, and may He forever bless America. Black America truly felt the full impact of the attack upon America. We also felt the full impact of the attack upon us, even though we are also Americans. It is not easy being black in America because we are not always treated fairly in this country, but it is not enough to keep us from progressing toward a better America for black America. We have got to keep our heads up during hard times. After all, blacks live through days like 9/11 almost every single day.

CHAPTER 15

MODERN DAY LYNCHING

Psalm 142:6 "Hear my cry, for I am very low. Rescue me from my persecutors, for they are too strong for me." Racism has evolved into the 21st century. Once there was Jim Crow laws in which over time have become illegal and outdated. Now Jim Crow has evolved to James Crow. Lynching has become more modernized, but yet very much as effective as Jim Crow.

Under the new name of "James Crow", rich, famous, and successful blacks who break any kind of law or mores, this black person is unduly ridiculed and put in his or her "place". They are reminded that under the newly established James Crow law that even though they are rich and successful, a black person will never be equal.

Through my experiences with white America is that they seem to become offended whenever the subject of racism is mentioned by a black person. Racism seems to make whites very uncomfortable, and it should, even to the point of anger. Some totally deny that racism exists in America and that blacks get more than their fair share of what this country has to offer. None of this is, by any stretch of the imagination, close to the truth. This is their way of justifying a well-known, outright lie.

There are laws in place to protect us from wrongdoings in America. However, when it is a black offender of the law, he or she, in most cases, is prosecuted much more harshly than the white offenders who break the same law. We are then subjected to the unwritten law of James Crow. For example, New York Giant rich and famous wide receiver, Plaxico Burress, had a registered, concealed gun in a New York nightclub. The gun went off, shooting Mr. Burress in the leg. He accidentally shot himself, but since the gun was registered in the state of Florida and not New York he was indicted on a gun charge. It mattered not that there were no victims other than himself. He consequently received three (3) years penitentiary time, and he is not even a criminal.

Another example of injustice for black athletes is Michael Vick. Michael Vick is by no means a criminal. Due to his boyhood pastime (which was fighting dogs), he continued to enjoy what he thought was a legitimate pastime. He even said that the police would often pass by his neighborhood, get out of his patrol car, and watch the dog fights; but when the police was satisfied by the fact that no humans were involved, he would get back in his patrol car and drive off. Can you now understand why he continued to fight dogs as an adult? Truth: During the civil right struggle, dogs were turned loose on black human beings, and nothing was said. Now dogs have more rights than blacks.

Allow me to test your love for animal. Let us say that Michael Vick abused 20 innocent dogs. Let's say Michael Vick lost a small sum of $100 million for his actions. So, it's safe to say that comes to $5 million per dog victim. Be honest. No one knows what you are thinking, but how many of you will go home, call your pet, rub him or her a few times, then choke your sweet little pet to death for $5 million in cold cash? I am willing to bet that you wouldn't even care who witnessed this act. You would drown your pet on national television for $5 million.

Michael Vick was not sentenced for what he did to those dogs. He was sentenced for being black with millions of dollars. Joe the Plumber would only have been sentenced to 30 days in jail and a $5000 fine. For 20 dogs that's about $250 per dog. No one but a crack head would kill their pet for $250. I am merely trying to point out the reasonable value of a dog versus Michael Vick's race and net worth. Do you deem it reasonable to take away life's necessities from Michael Vick's children for a dog's ransom? Is it fair to deprive a man of making a living for his family for killing some dogs? Yes, Vick should have been punished for his involvement; but who determines the value of a dog's life to be $5 million?

Gilbert Arenas, guard for the Washington Wizards, was charged with having an unloaded gun in his team locker room at the Verizon Center.

Arenas was suspended from the NBA for the rest of the year and faces up to six months in prison. He is being charged with felony weapon possession and stands to lose over $80 for his bad judgment. Commissioner David Stern called it "an education lesson for others." This makes one wonder what "others" he's referring to.

Michael Jackson was acquitted on child molestation charges, but he was sentenced to death because he could not handle the pressures of the media mob. He was lynched not by the old way of the rope, but he was hung by the depression of media madness. By succumbing to the preferences of society (Hollywood in particular), Michael Jackson deliberately changed his skin color, nose and hair, but he still discovered in the end what was real -- he was black.

Barry Bonds, the homerun king of Major League Baseball and will be until someone breaks his record. Barry's spectacular feat is marred by rumors of steroids use. He was forced out of baseball, which is another form of modern day lynching. He will never receive proper recognition for is hall of fame career.

Mike Tyson was doomed when Cuz DiMaggio died. Tyson became ripe for the pickings by the media lynch mob. He was charged and convicted of rape by a young woman who voluntarily came to his hotel room at 1:00 a.m. Mike Tyson was young, rich, and well known. However, he was not very smart to know that he was being measured for lynching. Tyson became yet another rich, black man to loose millions of dollars.

Another victim of the James Crow law was Serena Williams, the number one women's tennis player in the world. Serena was recently fined the largest fine in tennis history. Is this a coincidence? I think not. Remember when John McEnroe had temper tantrums, throwing his tennis racquet all over the place? Remember when he cursed the judges vehemently, calling them everything but a child of God; but he was never fined half as much as Serena Williams. Being one of many tennis brats, she offended (not threatening her life) the line judge. Serena apologized to all involved, but still she was fined a record amount of $92,000. Serena did not pay millions; but to the gallows, she stood for lynching.

Tiger Woods is a poster case for the James Crow lynching, for he was guilty of adultery multiple times with multiple women. His real crime is being black, rich, and famous, and the best damn golfer in the world. Tiger did not owe the world an apology. He only owed God and his wife an apology, but the rules change when it comes to us. For instance, a man can cheat on his wife and still be president of the United States. Who died and made Tiger Woods a god? He is only a man, and he made a sorrowful mistake. David Letterman admitted to multiple affairs and was not nearly as persecuted as Tiger Woods. In fact, it became comical on his show because he said he didn't discriminate with whom he cheated. Letterman was spared being lynched while Tiger has to meet his fate -- lynching. Again, another famous black has lost a great deal of money. Only this time it's hundreds of millions.

This is only a few examples of the many racial injustices in America. It is ten times as bad for indigent blacks, but the media hardly ever covers their stories. We as blacks need to take heed to the aforementioned cases and realize that we are not exempt from James Crow. It was demonstrated in Houston, Texas by criminology researchers that blacks were receiving much stiffer sentences for the same crimes and having the same criminal histories as the white boys. I am by no means implying that all those black athletes mentioned are not guilty of something, but the punishment exceeds the crime.

If you find the James Crow concept hard to understand, simply follow the money trail. The millions of dollars that Michael Jackson spent on attorney fees alone could have been put to much better use. Another example is Michael Vicks' million that went to the people who cared for the dogs after his arrest was unjustified. How much was the dog food and the hands that fed the dogs (volunteers) cost? After all, Michael Vicks' children are victims too.

CHAPTER 16

PRESIDENT BARACK HUSSEIN OBAMA

President Barack Obama was born an American citizen in 1961. His mother is a white American, and his father is a native of Kenya. His father was educated at Harvard while President Obama received his degree from Columbia University where he majored in political science. He later attended Harvard and graduated magna cum laude and served as first African American president of Harvard Law Review. Even as a young college student, Barack gained the attention of many white Americans. Little did anybody know his journey had just begun.

Even though his mother is white, he is considered black. He became a civil rights attorney in Chicago, Illinois and taught at the University of Chicago Law. He then became an Illinois state senator from 1996 till 2004, receiving 70 percent of the vote. White America began to pay even more attention to this young, successful black man.

Barack Obama was elected as president of the United States of America on November 4th, 2008. He received more votes than the Arizona senator, John "The Maverick" McCain. After a close race against Hillary Rodman Clinton for the democratic presidential nomination, he became the 44th United States president as well as the first African American president.

It was a very proud day for black people all over the world. However, President Obama received many votes outside the black race. This day we will never forget as long as we live. President Obama set the bar high for our black youth, but not out of reach. Every person in America can tell you just where they were when the election results were announced to the world. People of all races cried while embracing one another. A day that will be remembered in American history.

Blacks love America as much as whites love America. However, it is very hard to identify with white Americans when white Americans neglect to recognize black contributions to America. We should be one country, one government, and one people. "And if a house becomes divided against itself, that house will not be able to stand." (Mark 3:25).

What makes this presidency so great is that the black man in America has been the hardest worked, most hated, most discriminated against, and the most victimized by theft; and, yet, he became the most powerful man in the United States of America. I know there's a God. The black race as a whole has had to work harder and be above average before the average white person would even consider them for any respectable job. Barack Obama came fully loaded with qualifications. In my opinion, he was overqualified in the sense that white people felt uncomfortable for the simple fact that Barack was such a rarity. The previous president was academically average, and that's being generous. Then along comes an upper class black man with a nuclear family who lives in a million dollar home, and he didn't get where he was by selling drugs. He played by the dominant group's rules and worked hard for everything he had.

I am reminded of a song. In fact, it was often used during Obama's campaign. The words are: It's been a long time coming, but a change is going to come". I am fully convinced that that change could not have come about without God. I first give God the glory, for I believe that he was tired of the lying, stealing, misleading, killing, and all the rest of the illegal activity that was taking place in America prior to November 4th, 2008.

A special acknowledgement needs to be given to the millennial generation, also known as generation X. This group consists of young people between the ages of 18 - 29. The millennial group, according to Pew Research Center, has been the most consequential group of adults for the last few years. In fact, they make up over half the population in the western world. Unlike their parents, the baby boomers, this group of young people are more democratic, more tolerant of different arrangements (same-sex marriage and interracial marriage). Whether or not one agrees with their "live and let live" philosophy, Barack Obama would not and could not have become president without their vote. These young people are also the most technologically astute group, which made them an asset to the campaign itself because they were able to transmit information via internet within seconds. They made the difference.

I think it's important to give credit where credit is due, for Obama could not have accomplished the presidency without white people. Fair white people have been the earthly saving grace for black people throughout history. There was always some "good" white folk around to speak up for the abolition of slavery, to use their homes as stopping points for the underground railroad. John Brown even gave his life for what he believed in.

I pray that God would continue to bless America. We should all pray for our country as well as its leaders. Give Obama a fair amount of time to live up to his promises. After all, he knew that the road wouldn't be easy; but he said that he would not quit. I believe him. He won't quit, and God won't quit. This nation has got to live up to the true meaning of the *Constitution*. No terrorists will destroy America. America can only be destroyed from within. God bless America.

Conclusion

Success is not a birthright and neither is being poor. How we live in America mostly depends on the decisions we make in life. It is not always easy for black Americans to get what this country has to offer, but I assure you that it is not impossible.

Education is the key to success. Even though everyone is not college material, the ones who are college material can contribute greatly in lifting up the submerged masses. W.E.B. Dubois wrote *The Education of Black People*. This book contained Dubois' critiques about education and black people that ranged from 1906 - 1960. For over half a century, Dubois studied the lack of education of black people and came up with the same conclusions that apply today.

> What is needed for any group of advancing
> people is the college-bred community, for
> no matter how far the college may fail in individual
> cases it is, after all, the center where knowledge of
> the past connects with the ideal of the future. Every

community, therefore, must be college-bred; and that
does not mean that every individual must be a college
graduate; it may be that the proportion of college-bred
men may be small, even infinitesimal; and still the
community, by tradition and heritage, will hold fast
to what the past has taught the world of high and ideal
future accomplishments. But, given a group or community
which don't know the message of the past and
does not have within its own number, the men who can
feel it, and is separated from contact with outside groups
who can teach it -- given such a community and you have
a desperate situation which calls for immediate remedy.

America's black students, especially the south, have the lowest academic test scores in the country. We are not deficient, but we do put our priorities in the wrong places. It has been demonstrated that blacks spend more money on clothing than any other race. This is not something to embrace and be proud of. Parents, we need to bathe our children in education and everything that is consistent with economic upward mobility.

Why are the expectations of black men so low. It is because that has been what was mainly demonstrated. It is the same reason that the Los Angeles Lakers fan expect to win the NBA championship every year. Their basketball team has clearly, undeniably demonstrated that they are the best in the most recent years. Many black men have demonstrated through their absence that they are unproductive, absent parents, and citizens who scare other blacks, let alone whites.

In black neighborhoods it is typical for black youngsters and some who aren't so young to stand on the corner under the street light, wear pants below the hips, have unkempt hair and a vocabulary that the average nonblack person cannot understand. It has been proven that blacks who never move out of the "hood" are moving farther and farther away from mainstream America.

I have to admit that blacks were never expected nor intended to succeed in America. The plan was to be slaves so that the white males and their families could live a live of leisure, but that was then. This is now. We can accomplish anything that our minds can conceive and believe. We can reverse the expectations of white America by reversing our actions, educational achievements, parenting skills, and, most of all, expectations of ourselves. Thurgood Marshall expected to make changes in the legal system for the betterment of blacks. President Obama expects to even the health care insurance benefits for all Americans. Lastly, I expect to help somebody with the reading of this book. I close my book now, but I will never close my mind! Think about all that I have said throughout this book, and expect the best.

ACKNOWLEDGEMENTS

I was born and raised in DeQuincy Louisiana which is a small town where oppression for blacks is normal; blacks won't stand up for themselves or for their children. We have a new black council woman, Andrea Coleman Williams and DeQuincy needs to support her so that she can leave her legacy.

In acknowledgement of my grandsons, Khamryn, Christian, Jordan, and Kaden: my granddaughters, Paris, Taneisha, Gemma, Ebonee, Kyra, Yazmyn, Jada, Jaden and Alexsandra

I would also like to mention my many brothers and sisters. My living brothers are Sherman Lee, Leroy, Jr., and Marvin Keith.

My living sisters are Mittie and Josline Rigmaiden, Annie Marie, Dorenda Kay, Ida Louise, Kathy Marlene, and Kim Michelle.

In memory of my grandfather, Humphrey Warner; my cousins, Elizabeth "Niece" Tanner and Demetric "Dee-Dee" Tanner; my uncles S.M. Warner, Henry Warner, Humphrey Warner, Jr. Uncle Tim Smith, Uncle Thornton and Aunt Doris.

In memory of my brothers, Billy, Tommy, and Larry Rigmaiden.
In memory of my sister, Geraldine Rigmaiden Cole.
In memory of my father-in-law Mr. Irvin Toliver.

There are so many people who have been a big part of my life and a small part of my recovery. I would first of all like to thank God for keeping me strong in my many times of need. There is not any way possible for me to mention every friend, co-worker, or family member. I would like to say at this time that I am sorry if anyone feels left out of my book. Here are some of those who come to mind who have inspired me in some way: my mother-in-law Vinnie Broussard Toliver, whom I love very much as my own mother; my mentor, Mr. Wesley Wells. I would like to thank Mr. Wells for his love and concern for my well-being. I just hope I didn't let him down in any way. Again, I say thank you very much.

Last, but certainly not least, my cousins Mark Warner, Kevin Warner, Cheryl Warner, Karen Warner, Jennie Tanner, Wanda Jean Smith, Tim Walker; and my friends, Linda Dixon-Nelson and Gayle Brown.

www.ingramcontent.com/pod-product-compliance
Lightning Source LLC
Chambersburg PA
CBHW030402290526
45785CB00004B/1871